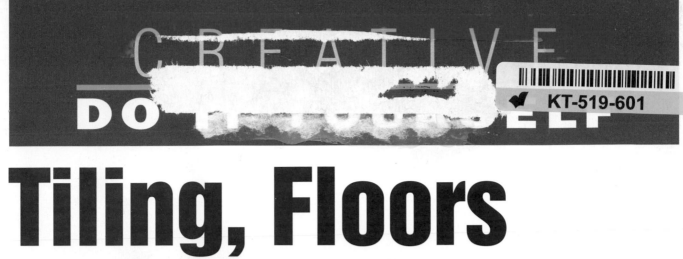

CREATIVE
DO IT YOURSELF

Tiling, Floors and Flooring

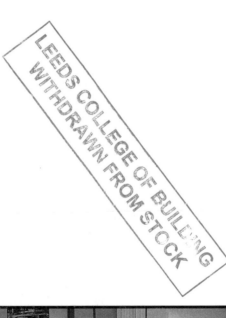

WARD LOCK

CONTENTS

INTRODUCTION

TILING, both on walls and ceilings, and laying new floorcoverings are often seen as decidedly tricky home-improvement jobs. However, advances in product technology have made the materials involved much easier to use than they used to be and this book provides all the information you need to tile walls and floors confidently, and to lay a variety of other floorcoverings.

The book begins with ceramic tiles for walls and worktops. It opens with a guide to choosing and buying the tiles and also describes the various materials – adhesive, grout, sealants, edging strips and other accessories – that are needed for the job. It explains how to estimate quantities, and how to use patterned and border tiles to create attractive decorative effects. It then describes how to tile a small area such as a splashback – the ideal project for a beginner since you can learn all the basic skills on a small scale. The book goes on to explain what is involved in tiling entire walls, where accurate planning and setting-out are the keys to success. The last two projects in this section show you how to tile a kitchen worktop and how to work with mosaic tiles.

The next section moves on to laying floor tiles – whether ceramic, cork, carpet or vinyl. Although the basic techniques needed for each material are similar, there are important differences. Each type is dealt with in detail, with illustrated step-by-step instructions as well as helpful problem solver panels to steer you in the right direction when the unexpected occurs.

Many people are nervous of laying sheet flooring, afraid of ruining a large piece of expensive material by cutting in the wrong place. Yet once you have mastered the principles involved, the task is surprisingly simple. This book contains detailed explanations of how to lay out, trim and fit both fitted carpet and sheet vinyl flooring in awkward corners and around obstacles. It also shows you how to use templates – the only effective way of laying sheet flooring in awkward rooms such as bathrooms where washbasin pedestals, WCs and bidets make accurate fitting difficult to achieve.

Finally, the book looks at wood floors and explains how to lift and repair existing floorboards as preparation for laying a new covering or to leave the boards on view and how to sand and seal the boards. Next, there are step-by-step instructions on laying new wood mosaic panels and woodstrip flooring, and on how to finish the new floor so that it looks good and wears well.

The final project is boarding a loft – a simple yet valuable improvement that provides extra storage space and eliminates the risk of putting a foot through the ceiling when moving about in the loft.

BUYING CERAMIC WALL TILES

Ceramic wall tiles, as their name suggests, are for use on walls only. They are too thin for floors or worktops (where tiles need to withstand heat and the occasional heavy load), and since they are not frost-proof they cannot be used outdoors. Wall tiles are fine, though, for tiling small ledges and other surfaces where heat and heavy loads are unlikely to be a problem.

Tile sizes

Wall tiles come in a variety of sizes, most of which are now metric (see chart below). The difference between metric and Imperial is only critical when you're matching existing tiling. The smallest size is 100×100mm, below which tiles are classed as mosaics and come on backing sheets. The largest DIY size is 300×200mm, though larger sizes are available.

Small tiles are usually thinner, and so easier to cut. But there's no need to be afraid of using larger tiles; even in a small room, they look nowhere near as daunting on the wall as they do in your hands.

The chart (right) shows the common sizes of wall tile currently available. The figure beside each size gives the approximate number required per square metre allowing

for 2mm joints and 5% wastage.

Most British-made tiles are sold in boxes of 25 or 50. Continental ones come by the square metre or in boxes of 18 or 36. It takes a lot of tiles to cover a relatively small area, so bear this in mind when you go to buy, and be careful when lifting.

Common Sizes	Coverage per sq m
100×100mm (about 4×4″)	100
108×108mm (4¼×4¼″)	87
150×150mm (about 6×6″)	44
152×152mm (6×6″)	43
150×200mm (about 6×8″)	34
200×200mm (about 8×8″)	25
200×300mm (about 8×12″)	16

Shopping for tiles

Most wall tiles are machine-made, which makes them much cheaper than hand-made ones. Hand-painted tiles are very expensive too.

It is worth shopping around for tiles. You may find some ranges selling at a big discount because they have been discontinued, or imported at a bargain price.

Superstores and builder's merchants stock only the most popular ranges, but you can usually take the tiles home straight away.

Specialist tile suppiers are growing in number and carry far more extensive ranges. Most offer free advice, though you may have to wait a few days for your order. A good supplier will always encourage you to order on the generous side (to allow for mistakes and breakages) and then offer you a full refund for unused tiles.

Tile edges

Today, there are effectively only two choices:

British-style 'Universal' tiles have 'bevelled' edges that butt up against each other leaving grouting gaps in between; several tiles within each pack have one or two glazed edges for use on edges and corners.

Continental-style square edged tiles need to be laid with plastic spacers between them to stop their edges touching and form gaps for the grout. The edges are nearly always left unglazed, but you can finish them with one of the plastic trim strips described over the page.

In the past, some tile ranges included special tiles with either single (RE) or double (REX) rounded

Ceramic wall tiles come in all shapes and sizes, and in a range of surface finishes. Special tiles include narrow quadrants for sealing gaps, and insert tiles – shown here is a 150×150mm built-in towel holder.

edges. These are now only available in white, in a single size – 108×108mm. Also rapidly disappearing are tiles with built-in spacer lugs for the grout gaps.

Special tiles As well as square and rectangular tiles, you can get wall tiles with more elaborate decorative shapes and narrow, oblong border tiles for use as edgings. Some of these are intricately moulded and look very impressive, but they tend to be expensive.

Many tile ranges also include accessory tiles such as soap dishes and towel rail holders. These are sold individually.

Quadrant tiles are narrow rounded tiles used for sealing the gap created between a bath, basin or ledge and a tiled wall. They are usually sold in kits containing straight lengths, internal and external corners, and end pieces.

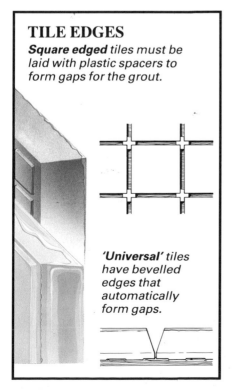

TILE EDGES

Square edged tiles must be laid with plastic spacers to form gaps for the grout.

'Universal' tiles have bevelled edges that automatically form gaps.

TILE ACCESSORIES

PLASTIC EDGING & SEALING STRIPS

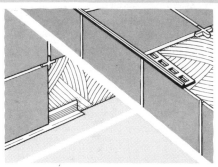

Plastic edging gives a neat finish to corners and edges where the tile edges are unglazed.

Sealing strip forms a watertight seal along the joints with worktops, baths and basins.

Both types are simply bedded in the tile adhesive before fixing the last row of tiles. They are sold in various lengths in a range of colours.

'TRUTILE' TILING GRID

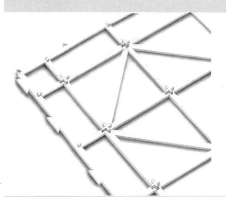

Ingenious system of plastic interlocking grids which are stuck to the wall with tiling adhesive or household glue. Small cross pieces within the grids then allow tiles to be spaced and levelled automatically. Obstructions are easily cut around with scissors or a knife.

Does away with the need for traditional setting out with battens, but can work out expensive on large areas, and only available for certain tile sizes.

FLEXIBLE SEALANT

Silicone or acrylic-based sealants used to fill gaps up to 6mm (¼″) wide between tiles and worktops or plumbing fixtures (sealants slump in wider gaps – use quadrant tiles or sealing strip instead). Also used in place of grout on tiled panels that need to be removed.

Best bought in cartridge form. Several colours are available; white quickly discolours.

WALL TILE ADHESIVE

Most wall tile adhesives are sold ready mixed in a range of different sized litre tubs. The standard type is PVA-based and only semi-water resistant; for walls prone to dampness or condensation (such as showers, bath splashbacks) use a water resistant acrylic-based adhesive. Acrylic-based adhesives also have better non-slip characteristics and some types can be used to grout the tiles as well; however, they are generally more expensive.

Cement based tile adhesive (more usual for floor tiling), can be used where the unevenness of the surface makes it necessary to apply a bed thickness of more than 3mm (⅛″). It comes in powder form in bags, and is mixed with water in a bucket.

Many tile adhesive ranges include a special surface primer, sold in cans, which reduces the risk of failure.

Cover guide: Ready mixed – 1sq m per litre; powder form – 1sq m per 3.5kg.

WALL TILE GROUT

Standard wall tile grouts come either ready mixed or in powder form. Ready mixed grouts are acrylic based and sold in tubs. Powder grouts are cement based, and come in bags for mixing with water; they are slightly easier to apply.

Both types are reasonably water resistant and can cope quite happily with showers or splashbacks. They cannot, however, take prolonged soaking (in a swimming pool, for example), and they are unsuitable for worktops since they can harbour germs. In situations like these, use a two-part epoxy resin grout – sold in a pack consisting of resin and hardener. This is impervious and non-toxic, but more expensive than standard grouts and much harder to apply.

Grouts are now available in a range of colours. Or, you can colour powdered grout with pigment additive.

Coverage guide: Ready mixed: 6–8sq m per kg. Cement-based: 1sq m per kg.

FIXING WALL TILES: PREPARATION

As any professional will tell you, the secret of successful wall tiling is to plan the job properly. Before you actually buy any tiles, you should be thinking about what sort of surface you'll be tiling on, and how to avoid fiddly cuts. And if you want to incorporate a design or pattern, it pays to work this out on paper first; mistakes made on the wall can be expensive!

WHAT YOU CAN TILE ON

There are no short cuts to preparing surfaces for tiling: they must be structurally sound, flat, dry, and free of dust and grease – otherwise the tiles won't stay up.

Wallpaper Definitely unsuitable. Strip it and treat the wall as below, depending on what you find.

Paint Start by making sure the wall is flat: remove any bumps on solid walls by bashing them with a hammer, and fill depressions over 3mm (⅛″) deep with general purpose filler. Pull out old wallplugs.

For gloss, rub down any flaky patches back to a sound surface, then rub over the entire area to provide extra grip for the adhesive. Finally, wash down with Sugar Soap to remove dust and grease.

For emulsion, it's essential that the paint itself is firmly stuck to the wall (see Tip). Rub down flaky or powdery paint and then seal with tile adhesive primer (available in cans from tile suppliers). Wash down sound paint with Sugar Soap.

Plaster Leave new plaster for at least a month before tiling. Seal all types of bare plaster with tile adhesive primer.

Plasterboard Fine, providing it is on a proper framework that doesn't allow it to flex. Treat as for paint or plaster, whichever is appropriate.

Old tiles Perfectly suitable so long as they're firmly fixed; remove any that aren't and level with filler. Rub over the surface with coarse silicon carbide paper to 'key' (scratch) the glaze, then wash down with Sugar Soap. Bear in mind that on old tiles the adhesive will take much longer to dry; you need to leave it at least 72 hours before grouting.

Wood Existing panelling is best removed as you can't guarantee it will remain stable. Hardboard panelling is totally unsuitable. New panelling should be at least 12mm (½″) thick and preferably in either blockboard or WBP (water and boil-proof) plywood. Using chipboard is risky, particularly in a bathroom; it swells when wet.

Panels must be supported every 300mm (12″) so that there is not the slightest chance of them flexing. Screw, rather than nail, them to the supporting framework. Paint **all** bare wood with an oil-based primer, preferably a couple of days before tiling, otherwise the adhesive may fail as it dries.

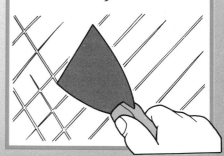

Trade tip

Know the score

❝ Tiles stick perfectly well to emulsion paint, but in my experience the paint itself often stops sticking to the wall – the tile adhesive softens it.

As a precaution against this happening, I always advise people to score the emulsion criss-cross fashion with the corner of a paint scraper, making the scores about 100mm (4″) apart. This way, the adhesive can penetrate and grip the plaster behind. ❞

TAILORING TILES TO YOUR HOME

Once tiles go on the wall they're there to stay, so think first about any other modifications you might want to make to the room.

Now is the time to install new electric cables and pipe runs, or hide any existing 'eyesores' behind boxed-in panels. At the same time, it's worth considering panelling in fixtures like a washbasin or bath so that you can tile over or around them as easily as possible.

The panelling doesn't need to be done to a high standard: it just has to be smooth and completely rigid. If you don't fancy tackling the work yourself it's better to get it done by a carpenter at this stage.

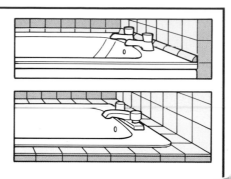

TILING AROUND A BATH

For a streamlined look, consider replacing the existing panel with a new tiled one.

First, work out how the bath should sit. Against tiled walls you can seal the join with quadrant tiles, sealing strip or silicone sealant, but if the bath has a ledge around it then it's better to tile the ledge as well and arrange for the lip of the bath to sit above the tiling.

This may involve moving the bath slightly or raising the height. On modern acrylic baths with screw-adjustable feet, there may be enough 'give' in the pipework to accommodate the move; if there isn't, get in a plumber to do the alterations.

Build the new panel frame out of 50×25mm (2×1″) softwood, anchoring it to the walls and floor, and allowing for a cross-brace every 300mm (12″). Don't forget to include the thickness of the tiles, adhesive bed and panelling in your calculations.

For the panelling, use 12mm (½″) WBP plywood or blockboard; make sure you sink all screws well below the surface.

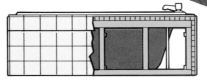

At least part of the main bath panel must be removable for access to the plumbing. Brace the back with extra battens to keep it rigid and fix it to the main framework with magnetic catches spaced every 600mm (24″).

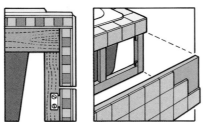

HALF TILED WALLS

Half tiled walls give you the practical benefits of tiled surfaces where you need them for less cost and work.

Make them look good by finishing the top course with contrasting decorative tiles, or with painted softwood dado or picture frame moulding. Alternatively, use plastic trims.

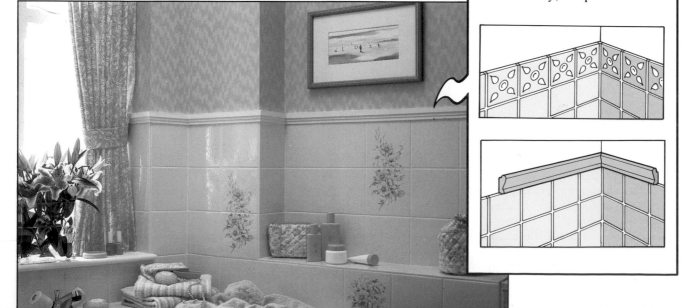

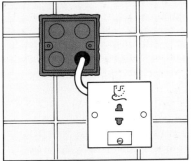

OBSTRUCTIONS AND SERVICES

Remove screw-on obstructions wherever possible – they can be fixed back later after tiling.

Shaver and power points look better if the tiling fits behind them, which means isolating the supply and loosening their fixing screws. If necessary, get an electrician to do this before you start tiling.

At the same time, think about adding or changing the positions of power points, and also about any new plumbing you want done. The cables and pipes must be laid before the tiles.

BOXING IN

Where possible, carry boxing for pipework or other fixtures to the nearest adjoining wall so that you aren't left with awkward nooks and crannies.

If this isn't feasible, make the box width match the width of the tiles you're using; this avoids fiddly cutting and helps the boxing blend in unobtrusively.

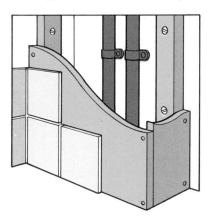

On smaller boxing jobs, there's no need for a frame – simply use butt-jointed panels of 19mm (¾″) blockboard or plywood, screwed together at the corners. Use battens or metal brackets where you need to secure the boxing to the wall.

DESIGNING WITH TILES

With the practical considerations out of the way, you can set about achieving the look that's right for your home.

Tile surfaces To a large extent the look of a tile depends on its glaze – gloss, satin, matt and lustre (mirror-like) are all available. Surfaces also vary, from smooth to textured.

Smooth, high-gloss tiles look best in a modern, streamlined decorative scheme. Matt-glazed textured tiles – many of which have a 'rustic' finish like old hand-made tiles – suit a country-style setting better.

Tile finishes As well as plain colours, wall tiles are produced in a range of 'effects' such as marble, water-splash and fabric stripe. All-over patterns tend to be more subdued and less fussy than they used to be; the modern trend is to use highly decorative tiles for borders only, or to mix them in with plain or lightly patterned tiles.

Designs and motifs

Most tile ranges now include motif tiles which you can place at intervals throughout a run for extra visual interest. Many also include special border tiles and interchangeable sets which, when laid together, form either a larger motif or a distinctive design.

The ultimate sets form complete pictures, and are known in the trade as 'panels'. Some are sold ready-boxed, others are made up to order. They are usually more expensive than plain tiles within the same range, so check before you buy.

You can also get tiles which co-ordinate with fabrics, and narrow oblong border tiles – often elaborately moulded and frequently hand painted.

Right A selection of motif and decorative tiles:
(A) Hand-painted decorative inset tile with frame. **(B)** Two styles of machine-made decorative tile with a printed hand painted effect. **(C)** Rustic effect machine-made motif and plain tiles. **(D)** Machine-made 'reproduction' motif and plain tiles.
Below Six-tile floral panel.

Trade tip

Don't skimp!

❝ As a tile supplier, I always advise people to think of tiles as they would wallpaper. This means buying enough tiles to do the whole job in one go: tiles vary in colour between batches, often dramatically, and there's no guarantee you'll get a match if you under-order.

Remember, too, that if your tiles have to match something else in the room, it's worth asking if you can borrow a few samples to try out at home. ❞

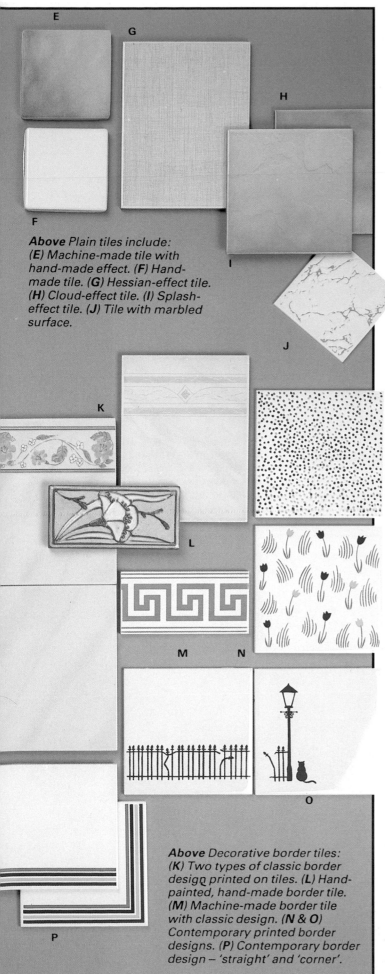

Above Plain tiles include:
(E) Machine-made tile with hand-made effect. **(F)** Hand-made tile. **(G)** Hessian-effect tile. **(H)** Cloud-effect tile. **(I)** Splash-effect tile. **(J)** Tile with marbled surface.

Above Decorative border tiles: **(K)** Two types of classic border design printed on tiles. **(L)** Hand-painted, hand-made border tile. **(M)** Machine-made border tile with classic design. **(N & O)** Contemporary printed border designs. **(P)** Contemporary border design – 'straight' and 'corner'.

Decorative borders are highly effective on half tiled walls. It's a good way to achieve a stylish look not too expensively, as plain tiles are generally cheaper.

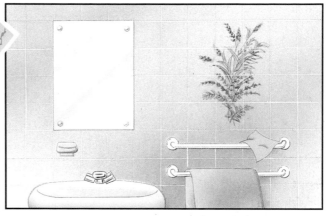

Position a tile panel as you would a picture, taking into account the proportions of the room, and the shape and position of nearby objects.

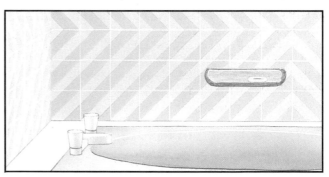

All over patterns give you considerable scope for experimenting, but make sure you finalize the design on paper before you begin fixing.

Random patterns using motif tiles can also look highly effective, especially if you incorporate a panel which picks out one of the motifs as a focal point.

The vast range of tiles available opens up some exciting and unusual design possibilities.

■ **Varying the layout** Instead of a conventional horizontal layout, consider fixing the tiles diagonally in 'diamonds'. As well as being strikingly effective, it can often make a small room seem larger.

■ **Designs and patterns** Handling motif tiles and multi-tile panels with bold designs needs care and fore-thought. For best results, draw a scale plan of the wall as shown, then try out different layouts. (Keep the plan handy to use as a fixing guide.)

As a general rule, position a panel like you would a picture, taking into account the proportions of the wall and any nearby fixtures.

Another tip is to avoid locating any sort of motif tile near the edges of the wall – if you have to cut tiles, the design may be spoiled. Also, allow *at least* 10 plain tiles for every motif or panel tile, otherwise the effect is much too fussy.

■ **Decorative borders** Use decorative borders as the last course on a half tiled wall or wherever there are strong visual 'lines' in the room – for example, around a splashback, along the front of a built-in basin, or around the bath.

■ **Built-in mirrors** Instead of hanging framed mirrors or screwing cut mirror to the wall, consider ordering one or two large mirror tiles – commonly available up to 2ft (600mm) square – and having them cut to a multiple of your tile size (ordinary mirror glass has too fragile a backing to be glued). You can then fix the mirror tiles flush with the wall and grout around them.

ESTIMATING QUANTITIES

The safest way of estimating quantities is to draw a plan of each wall and section off the main areas as shown. Find the total area first, multiplying the height by the width. Then find the areas of the sections that won't be tiled and subtract them from the total. Count motif tiles and panels tile by tile.

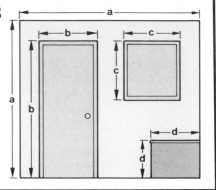

INCORPORATING A TILE DESIGN

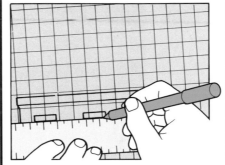

1 Draw a plan of each section of wall to be tiled (including any boxing in) on some 5mm squared paper, if possible making each square the equivalent of one whole tile. Do the plan in pencil first, then ink it in.

2 Using a pencil again, draw in your proposed design on the plan tile by tile. See how it looks, and if necessary try out different patterns or positions. Then, when you're happy, ink it in and keep it as a reference for when you tile.

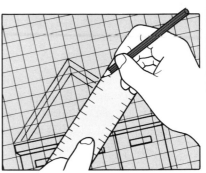

Above *A finished plan, showing a simpler variation on the design used in the kitchen (left).*

FIXING WALL TILES: SPLASHBACKS

Thanks to modern tools and materials, fixing wall tiles has become one of the most satisfying and rewarding of all decorating jobs. But if you've never done any tiling before – or you have, but it hasn't worked out too well – it's best to start with a small area like a kitchen splashback or bath surround.

This gets you used to working with tiles without the extra complication of setting out and battening the walls – techniques which are covered on pages 19-22.

Tools for the job

After you've prepared the surface and dealt with any obstructions, the next stage is to get together a set of tiling tools.

Tile cutter For tiles up to around 150 × 200mm (6 × 8″), buy an inexpensive cutting set consisting of a measuring jig/cutting guide, and a combined cutting wheel/tile snapper; you'll find this easier to use than the old method of scoring and snapping tiles over a matchstick.

For larger (and therefore thicker)

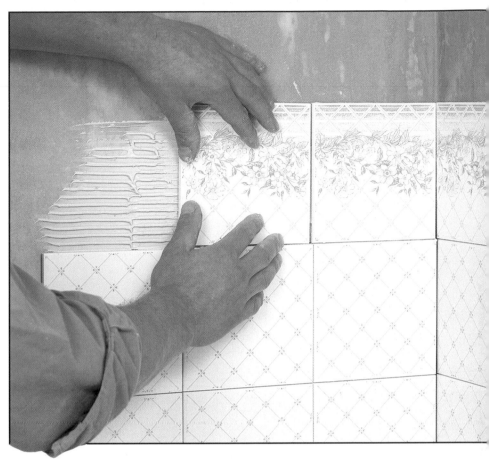

.... Shopping List ....

Plain tiles Divide surfaces to be tiled into rectangles, measure areas and combine; add 5% for breakages and waste.

Motif/border tiles Plan individual designs on squared paper; use this to estimate quantities and as a positioning guide.

Edging strip Measure exposed edges around tiled area; choose strip colour to complement or contrast with tiling.

Quadrant tiles Measure total length required; kits include corner and end pieces.

Sealing strip Normally sold in 1.8m (6′) lengths.

Spacers For spacing non-universal tiles; to estimate quantity, multiply number of tiles required by 1.5. .

Adhesive For wall tiles, average coverage is 1 litre per sq m.

Grout – for 2mm spacing, average coverage is 0.15kg per sq m.

Tools checklist Tile cutter, tile edge sander, adhesive and grout spreaders, spirit level, tape measure, bucket, sponge.

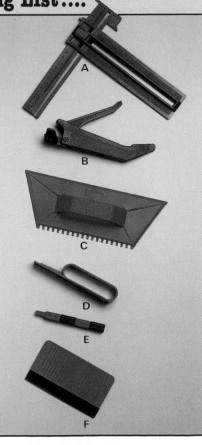

tiles, or if you plan to do any floor tiling, invest in a proper cutting jig; these make light work of even the toughest tiles. (Some tile suppliers have jigs available for hire.)

Tile edge sander An inexpensive tool which smooths the edges of cut tiles and makes all the difference to the finish; the abrasive pads are replaceable.

Adhesive and grout spreaders A notched adhesive spreader is a must: the furrows it creates aid suction, helping the tiles to stick. Sometimes spreaders are supplied with the adhesive, otherwise buy one. Just as important is a rubber bladed grout spreader for spreading and removing excess grout.

Grout joint finisher A cheap plastic tool for rubbing grout joints to a smooth finish. Alternatively, use a piece of 6mm (¼″) wooden dowel (*don't* use your fingers).

A typical set of tiling tools for small-scale jobs: tile jig and cutting guide (A), combined cutter/snapper (B), notched adhesive spreader (C), edge sander (D), four-stage grouting tool (E) and grout spreader (F).

SETTING OUT

For a splashback or bath surround only a few rows high, there's normally no need to bother with traditional supporting battens. However, you *must* have a firm, level surface – such as a worktop or bath edge – to use as a base.

Your aim should be to place the tiles where they look easiest on the eye, and to avoid unsightly cuts. Usually, this means finding the middle of the wall, and then tiling outwards from here so that any gaps at the ends are the same width.

However, narrow gaps look ugly, so you need to decide now whether to start tiling *on* the midpoint, or *to one side* of it. The illustrations on the right show how to do this for three common situations – either by laying out the tiles in a 'dry run', or measuring along the wall in tile widths. (In both cases, don't forget to allow for 2mm (1/16") for the grout if the tiles are square edged.)

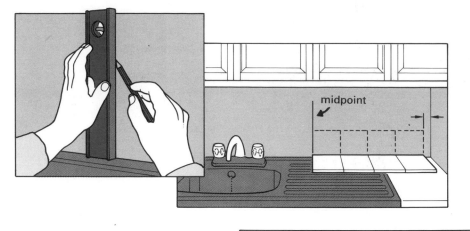

Find the midpoint by measuring the wall, then draw a vertical line using your spirit level (above). The line isn't strictly necessary, but it makes it easier to align the tiles when you come to fix them.

Lay out a row of whole tiles in a dry run, starting from one side of the midpoint (above right). If the gap at the end of the wall is too narrow, fix the tiles with the first tile centred over the midpoint instead (right).

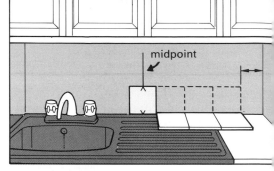

FIXING TILES

Spread out the adhesive and fix tiles in 'blocks' of roughly one square metre, working *along* the wall.

If you're using sealing strip at the bottom, or finishing strip at the top, remember to bed this into the adhesive before fixing the adjoining row of tiles (if it won't stay put, tack it in place temporarily with a couple of nails). With sealing strip, you might find you have to apply the adhesive quite thickly to take up the lip at the back.

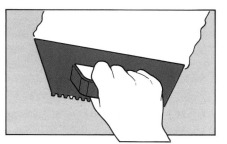

1 Using the back of your spreader, scoop the adhesive out of the tub and press it against the wall to one side of (or on) the midpoint.

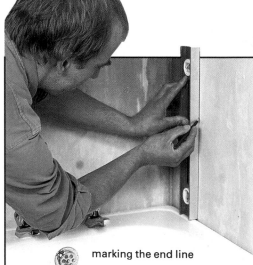

marking the end line

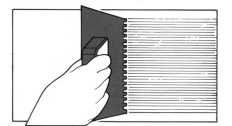

2 Gripping the spreader as shown, spread the adhesive in an even layer 2-3mm (1/16") thick. Apply enough to cover roughly 1 sq m (1 sq yd) of wall.

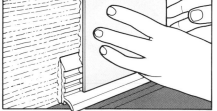

3 If you're using sealing strip, bed this into the adhesive. Then grip the first tile between your fingers and press it gently on to the wall.

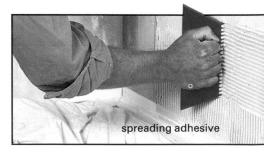

spreading adhesive

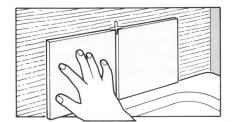

4 Having checked the tile sits square to the base or strip, bed spacers into the adhesive top and bottom and position the next tile in the same way.

5 Continue spacing and fixing, making sure the tiles engage the spacers. Stop every so often and check with your level that the tiles are sitting flush.

fixing subsequent tiles

For a basin splashback,
mark the midpoint as
shown on the previous
page and then see which
layout looks best by
marking off in whole tile
widths. Don't let the tiles
overhang the edge of the
basin too far: they won't
have sufficient support.

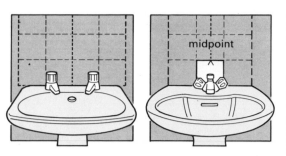

Around a bath, plan things
so that any cut tiles on the
end wall(s) are in the
corner, allowing you to
finish on whole tiles. (If
necessary, let the tiles
overhang the bath slightly
so the cut tiles aren't too
narrow.) Having worked
out the layout, draw a
vertical line where the
whole tiles end to use as a
guide when fixing.

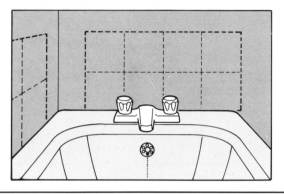

Trade tip

Start level
❝ If you're unlucky, the worktop
or bath you're tiling above has
an upstand or moulded edge
which makes it impossible to
'sit' the first row of tiles.

In this case, you have to fix up
a support batten. Nail it to the
wall a tile's height above the
base, making sure it is level;
leave the nail heads protruding,
for easy removal.

Tile above the batten in the
usual way then, when the tiles
have set, remove the batten and
fill in the bottom row. ❞

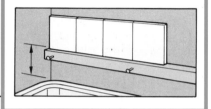

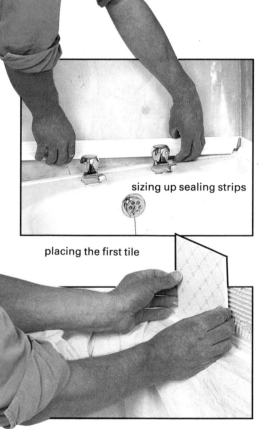

sizing up sealing strips

placing the first tile

using a cutting jig

CUTTING TILES

On a splashback or bath surround
there should be no need for
anything other than straight cuts.
Marking and cutting awkward
shapes is covered on pages 19-22.
Tile cutting jigs like the one shown
have a built-in marking gauge which
you set to the width of the gap prior
to cutting. However, this assumes
the wall is square – which it often
isn't – so double check by
measuring the gap top and bottom,
allowing for the grout.

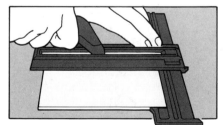

1 Check that the space for a cut
tile is square by measuring it
top and bottom. If it is, set the jig
as shown; if not, transfer the
measurements to the tile.

2 For a square cut, simply lay
the tile in the jig. For an
angled cut, rule a line on the
glazed side in felt pen and align it
with the slotted cutting guide.

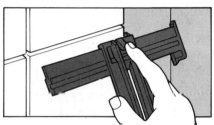

3 Holding the tile and jig steady
with one hand, place the
cutting tool in the guide and draw
it firmly towards you along the
slot. Keep the pressure even.

4 To break the tile, hold it as
shown and position the
snapping jaws of the cutting tool
directly over the cutting line;
squeeze gently to snap.

5 Without disturbing the
adhesive bed, check that the
cut piece fits. If it does, support
it, then smooth the edge with
your tile file.

GROUTING AND FINISHING

Leave the tiles to set for the time recommended by the adhesive manufacturers (normally at least 12 hours) before grouting.

If the grout is in powder form, add it to the specified amount of water in a bucket and mix to a smooth, but fairly stiff, consistency. If it's ready-mixed, stir in the tub and then apply direct to the wall.

Bear in mind that grouting is a messy job, so cover everything else before you start. Time is of the essence, since the grout hardens rapidly and becomes impossible to work into the joints, so make sure you have enough to do the job in one go. And – just as important – don't allow any grout to dry on the surface of the tiles; it's *very* difficult to remove once hard.

When you apply the grout, leave the joint along the adjoining surface clear (or scrape out the grout before it dries). Later, when the grout has set, fill the joint with silicone or acrylic sealant. This provides a flexible seal that won't disturb the tiles if there's any movement.

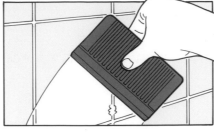

1 *Use your adhesive spreader to daub grout over tiles, then quickly work it over the surface and into the joints with the grout spreader.*

2 *Wipe away the excess with a sponge, washing it out frequently. Take care not to leave any ungrouted 'pin holes' between the joints.*

3 *When the grout has begun to harden, rub down the joints to smooth them off to an even width. Check for any stray grout still on the tiles.*

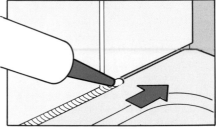

4 *Finally, seal any gaps along the adjoining bath edge or work surface with sealant. Remember to push the tube away from you.*

▌ PROBLEM SOLVER ▐

Tiles not flush

Check constantly while you are fixing to make sure all the tiles sit flush with one another. If one stands proud of, or below, the surface (and assuming you've prepared the surface properly), the problem is almost certainly that the adhesive bed is uneven at this point.

Remove the tile immediately by prising it from behind with an old kitchen knife, taking care not to disturb the others. Then scrape off **all** the adhesive from both surfaces, spread a fresh bed, and continue as before.

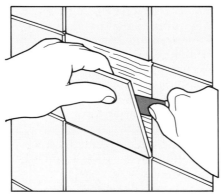

Ease the tile away *gently with a kitchen knife to break the suction of the adhesive bed.*

Use the kitchen knife *to scrape the tile. It's easier to clean down the wall with your spreader.*

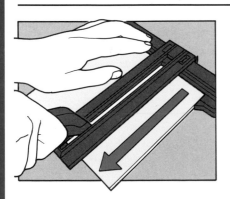

Draw the cutter towards you *in a single firm stroke when cutting tiles in a jig.*

Cutting problems

If your tiles aren't snapping cleanly when you cut them, it's probably because you are being too hesitant with the cutter. As with glass, you need to score in one firm, even pass so that the cutter's wheel penetrates the glaze to a consistent depth. If you hesitate, press too lightly, or go back over the same line more than once, you'll find yourself left with a jagged edge that no amount of filing or grouting can disguise.

Tiles slumping

If the tiles begin to slump downwards as you build up the rows, it means you've gone too far without arranging proper support. The method shown here relies on starting from a solid, level base and only fixing 4-5 rows in a single session. If you want to fix more, leave the first batch for at least 12 hours before continuing.

Unfortunately, the only cure for slumping is to start again before the adhesive dries.

FIXING WALL TILES: LARGE AREAS

Wall-tiling a whole room involves much the same fixing and cutting techniques as those described in the previous section. But this time you are working on a larger scale, which means taking a lot more care over the way you set out the job. Also, unless you're lucky, you'll find yourself having to cut and shape tiles to clear obstructions and awkward corners.

Tools and materials

In addition to the basic tiling tools listed on page 15, you need to make yourself a marking stick (see below). Also, because of the amount of cutting, it's worth hiring a professional-style cutting jig.

The best tool for cutting fiddly shapes in tiles is a tile saw (if you have a carpenter's coping saw, buy an Abrafile blade and use this instead). Sawing is far more efficient than the old 'score and nibble' method, though you must take care to support the tiles properly or they may crack.

If you plan to drill tiles, buy a special spear-shaped bit.

Apart from the usual tiling materials, get in a supply of wood for the support battens – 50×25mm (2×1″) is the ideal size, since it's light and easy to fix.

How the job runs

Setting out is the most crucial stage of tiling a whole room, and the one that many people get wrong.

Normally you'll be tiling to the floor or skirting, both of which are likely to be too uneven to use as a base. So your first job (shown below) is to draw a horizontal base line which allows every row of tiles to be level.

The next stage is to adjust your base line, depending on what's in the room, to avoid having to make unsightly cuts anywhere between floor and ceiling level.

From here you can judge where to place the setting out battens that support the rows of tiles above and keep them level. Having fixed all the tiles inside the battens, you then remove the battens and fill in the remaining gaps.

.... Shopping List ....

Tile materials checklist:
Plain tiles, motif and/or border tiles, edging strip (for borders and external corners), quadrant tiles (for finishing wide gaps), sealing strip (alternative to quadrant tiles), spacers (square-edged tiles only), adhesive (average coverage 1 litre/sq m), grout (covers 0.15kg/sq m).
Other materials:
Battens Buy enough wood to cover the length and height of the walls.
Nails For fixing battens (on a solid wall use masonry nails).
Tool checklist:
Tile cutting equipment, marking stick, tile sander, tile saw, adhesive and grout spreaders, spirit level, tape measure, bucket, hammer.

Right: Using a batten to check that the tiles lie flat.

DRAWING A BASE LINE

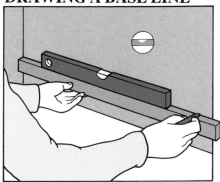

1 *Using a batten and spirit level, draw a level line right around the room just under a tile's width above where the tiles are to finish.*

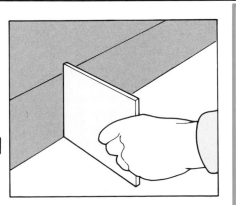

2 *Nowhere should the line be more than a tile's width above the finishing point. Check that this is so: if it isn't, draw a new base line lower down.*

Trade tip

Make your mark

❛ No tiler would be without his marking stick, a tool allowing him to gauge at a glance how many tiles fit between two points. To make one, take a piece of 50 × 25mm (2 × 1″) batten about 1.5m (4″) long and mark it off in whole tile widths; allow for the grout gaps if necessary. ❜

SETTING OUT THE ROOM

Setting out allows you to place cut tiles where they'll be least noticeable, and shows where to fix the support battens.

Start by using marking stick to measure the tile widths between the base line and any fixtures on the wall. Follow the sequence shown on the right, and mark where the cuts fall. Then adjust the height of the base line to get rid of cuts where you don't want them – for example along a window sill, or the top edge of the bath panel. Try to keep the cuts you *do* have to make even.

When you've done this, redraw the base line right around the room. This shows where to fit the horizontal support battens.

Use the same technique to check from side to side. Mark out each wall so that you avoid cut tiles at external corners and at the sides of windows. Where cuts are required at both ends of a wall, find its midpoint and measure out from here so that both lots are equal.

Finally, mark where the last column of whole tiles finishes on the left hand side of each wall. Plumb lines here, showing where to fix the vertical battens.

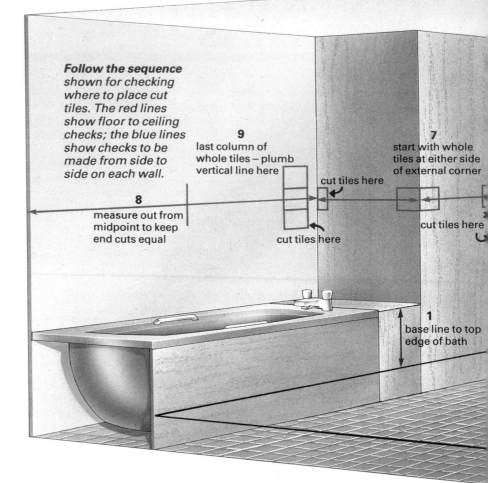

Follow the sequence shown for checking where to place cut tiles. The red lines show floor to ceiling checks; the blue lines show checks to be made from side to side on each wall.

9 last column of whole tiles – plumb vertical line here

7 start with whole tiles at either side of external corner

cut tiles here

cut tiles here

8 measure out from midpoint to keep end cuts equal

cut tiles here

1 base line to top edge of bath

TILING WITH BATTENS

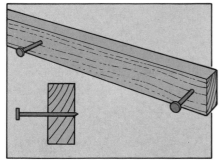

1 After marking your base line (previous page), part-drive nails into the first batten at 300mm (1') intervals; the points should just show through.

2 Offer up the batten level with the base line and drive in the nails until they hold; leave the heads protruding so you can remove the batten later.

3 Having evened up the cuts from side to side, draw a vertical line to mark the last column of whole tiles. Fix the side batten against this line.

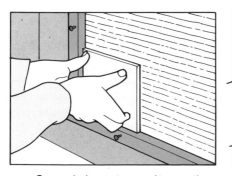

4 Spread about 1 sq m (1 sq yd) of adhesive in the usual way and fix the first tile in the corner of the two battens. Continue, working along the wall.

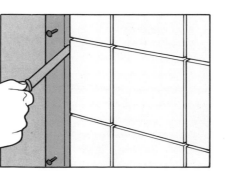

5 After completing the area inside the battens, leave it to set for an hour. Then slide a knife blade along the battens' edges to clear the joints.

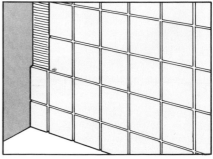

6 Remove the battens by pulling out the fixing nails with pliers. Measure and cut tiles to fit the gaps, and fix them in place in the usual way.

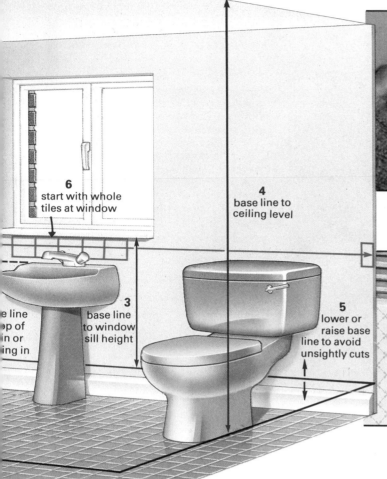

6 start with whole tiles at window

4 base line to ceiling level

3 base line to window sill height

line op of n or ing in

5 lower or raise base line to avoid unsightly cuts

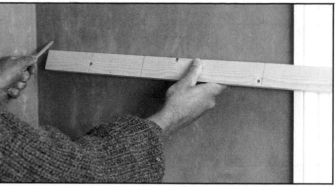

*A **marking stick** enables you to gauge the number of tiles – and cut tiles – in a run at a glance.*

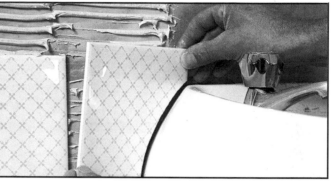

The way you arrange cuts around a basin is likely to be governed by prominent features – a window perhaps.

TILING AWKWARD AREAS

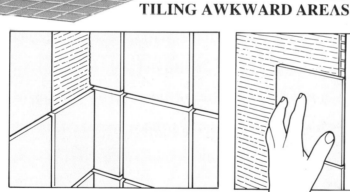

1 At internal corners, you overlap one set of cut edges with another. Work out in advance which way to arrange the overlap so it's least noticeable.

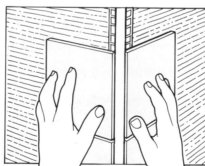

2 External corners can be finished with trim strip. Bed the strip in the adhesive, then simultaneously fix both 'columns' of tiles so you can align them.

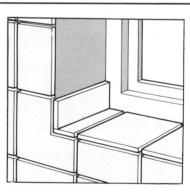

***Tile a window recess** after the main wall. Arrange for equal size cuts on either side.*

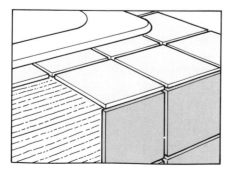

3 Alternatively, overlap tiles in the direction that's least noticeable. (Around a bath, tiles on a horizontal surface must overlap those on a vertical one.)

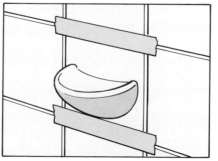

4 Give a heavy insert tile extra support by taping it to the neighbouring tiles. Use decorator's masking tape – you'll find it easier to remove later.

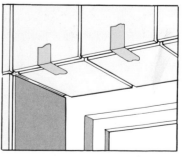

***Tackle the underside** last of all (the tiles on the wall above should overhang slightly to hide the edges). Tape the tiles for extra support.*

Tiling curved areas

Objects like a pedestal basin or soil pipe have large-radius curves that can be difficult to tile around. The answer is to make templates for each tile (see Tip), then mark and cut the tiles individually to fit. In most cases, the object will be symmetrical so you can use the templates twice – once for each side. Do the actual cutting with a tile saw.

When you come to fix the pieces of cut tile, you may find that the adhesive bed has thinned out around the obstruction. Allow for this by adding an extra dab of adhesive, press the tile home, and let the excess squeeze out around the edges. Scrape off immediately.

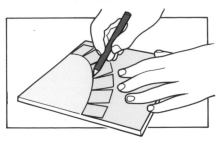

Use a paper template to mark the curve on each tile.

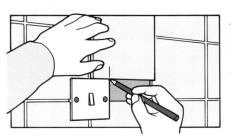

Add extra adhesive when you fit the cut piece.

—*Trade tip*—

Making a template

❝ I find the best way of making templates is the 'cut and tape' method. Cut some paper into tile size pieces, then cut strips about 12mm (½") wide in the sides. Press the paper 'tiles' against the object so that the strips fan out, describing the line of the curve. Afterwards, stick tape across them to hold the line; tear off the waste. ❞

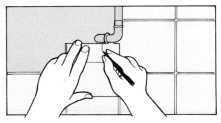

CUTTING AND SHAPING

A tile saw makes light work of cutting awkward shapes out of tiles, though you need to clamp them securely – use pieces of cloth to protect the surface glaze.

This leaves you with just one problem – marking the tiles to fit. Where possible, use something the same (or nearly the same) size as the object you're tiling around as a template (see step 5).

For pipes, don't attempt to cut all the waste out of one tile – it will break. Instead, cut the tile level with the centre of the pipe, then make equal sized cut-outs in each piece using a template.

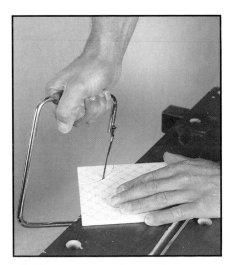

A tile saw cuts awkward shapes quickly and accurately – a lot more efficient than 'nibbling' the tiles with pincers. You may prefer to support a tile as shown.

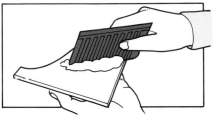

1 To mark a tile for an L shaped cut, start by holding the tile up to one side of the obstruction as shown and mark off against the edge with a felt tip pen.

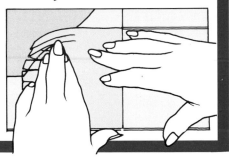

3 Having clamped the tile securely, cut down each line in turn using your tile saw. Take care not to stray past the corner where the lines join.

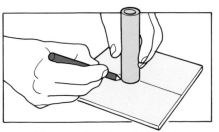

5 After cutting the tile, lay the two pieces together and mark the pipe cut-outs – preferably using an offcut of pipe of the same diameter.

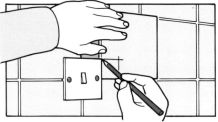

2 Now hold the tile against the other side of the obstruction and mark off again. Use your jig to convert the marks into squared cutting lines.

4 Use the same technique around a small pipe. Mark the pipe's position on a tile, then mark the tile for cutting level with the pipe's centre line.

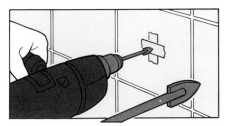

6 To drill holes in tiles, use a spade shaped tile bit and switch your drill to a low speed setting. Stick tape over your marks to stop the bit slipping.

TILING A
WORK SURFACE

Ceramic tiles make a stylish and extremely tough covering for work surfaces, being both heat and scratch-resistant. Laid properly – and over a sound enough base – there is no reason why a tiled worktop shouldn't last a lifetime. And the job itself is generally easier than tiling a wall, since you don't have the force of gravity to contend with.

The only drawbacks concern food preparation: you can't chop on tiles – they quickly blunt knives – and they are unsuitable for jobs such as pastry making which need a smooth, flat surface. Both problems can be solved, however, by using a wooden chopping board and marble slab, possibly inset in the tiled surface (see page 26)

Tiles for worktops

Tiles used for kitchen work surfaces must be a minimum of 5mm (¼") thick to be capable of withstanding hot, heavy pans and a lot of general wear and tear. This rules out most popular wall tiles – although wall tiles are of course perfectly suitable for tiling around a bath or vanity basin unit.

Instead, look to the thinner ranges of *floor tiles* for inspiration. Tile specialists (and to a lesser extent superstores) also stock ranges of purpose-made *worktop tiles* which include shaped upstand and edging tiles. Some ranges of *mosaic*

tiles are also thick enough, and at the top end of the market are *hand-made tiles*, though these can work out very expensive over a large area. A matt-glazed finish tends to look better on work surfaces than a high gloss one.

Size is largely a matter of personal preference, though tiles over 150mm (6") square are likely to be too unwieldy. The dimensions of the

Tiling is a practical finish for a work surface. In this family kitchen, the tiles are edged with hardwood to match the units, and continue up the splashback.

worktop could also affect your decision, since a sensibly chosen size can considerably reduce the amount of cutting you need to do. See overleaf for more details.

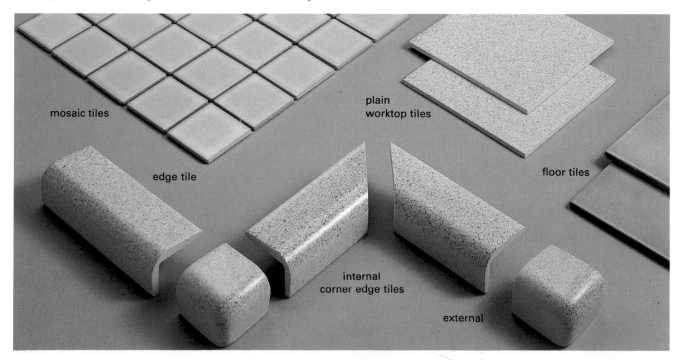

mosaic tiles

plain
worktop tiles

edge tile

floor tiles

internal
corner edge tiles

external

PLANNING THE JOB

The most important part of tiling a worktop is to provide a firm, level base which is also strong enough to take the weight of the tiles.

If you're starting from scratch, 12mm (½″) plywood or blockboard, or 19mm (¾″) chipboard are all suitable materials provided that boards are supported along their edges and at intervals of no more than 600mm (24″).

The following design points are also important:

■ If possible, size the worktop to multiples of your chosen tile size, to avoid fiddly cutting. This is especially important when using curved upstand and edge trimming tiles, where a row of cut plain tiles can spoil the effect.

■ Make the cut-out for a sink, hob, or other inset fitting before you start, then tile around it. The fittings themselves can sit over the tiles, though you may have to supplement their sealing gaskets with flexible sealant.

If tiling an existing worktop, make sure that it is strong enough. Most types of laminated worktop should be, but if the base is 12mm (½″) chipboard it's advisable to screw supporting battens to the underside.

You can also tile over an existing tiled surface, so long as the old tiles are firmly fixed. This gives you the option of using thinner tiles, but the combined thickness of the two layers could create problems with inset fittings.

■ It should be possible to tile around inset fittings *in situ* without removing any connections. Simply loosen the clip fixings below the worktop, cut around any sealant with a trimming knife, then prop the fittings on wooden wedges so that you can slip tiles under the lip.

■ Curved 'post formed' edges can be sawn off square or built up with a wooden lipping and filler.
■ Metal edging should be removed; wooden lipping is best tiled over.
■ Choose a tile size which results in the minimum of fiddly cutting.

Upstands can be formed with curved upstand tiles or plain tiles. Plain tiles are the better choice where there is any risk of movement between the worktop and wall.

Choose the tile size which best fits the worktop dimensions – or size the worktop to match the tiles, if you're starting from scratch.

Sockets and switches should be loosened from the faceplates before tiling around. Be sure to turn off the mains first.

Inset fittings can sit on top of the tiled surface. Use flexible sealant to supplement any sealing gaskets.

If using edge tiles, make sure there's enough clearance to open drawers. On thin worktops, they need the extra support of a batten glued and pinned along the edge.

Front edges can be finished with edging tiles or solid hardwood lipping or moulding. Wooden edging is a better choice for a post formed worktop, where edging tiles might be difficult to fit to the existing curved edge.

Lay tiles over an existing worktop, or on a base of plywood or blockboard.

.... Shopping List ....

Since worktops are seldom very large, it's worth drawing a scale plan to help you work out how many tiles to buy. A plan also allows you to plot the position of obstructions such as a hob, and to plan rows of cut tiles accordingly.

Use 5mm squared paper, letting each square represent a tile (2 or 3 squares if the tiles are rectangular).

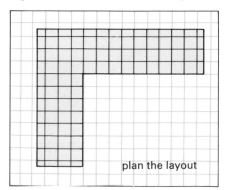

plan the layout

Edge and upstand tiles are half the width of plain tiles – count these individually off the plan. You should also add a few extra plain tiles, to allow for mistakes and breakages.

Adhesive for kitchen worktops should be the *thin-bed floor* type. This comes ready mixed or in powder form and covers around 2.75kg (6lb) per square metre.

Grout for work surfaces must at the very least be waterproof. On a kitchen worktop, it's best to use *epoxy grout* which is stain resistant and cannot harbour germs. Epoxy grout comes in two-part form, and unlike conventional grout is applied with a spatula. Coverage is in the region of 3–5sq m per kg depending on the tile size.

Edging timber should be hardwood lipping or moulding. It should be wide enough to finish flush with the tiles while completely covering the worktop edge.

Other materials you may need include *flexible sealant* and 50×25mm (2×1″) battens for setting out.

Worktop tiling tools
The thicker tiles used for worktops aren't so easy to cut as wall tiles, so use a *tile cutting jig* for straight cuts, and a *tile saw* for more awkward shapes. You also need a *tile sander* for finishing any cut edges, and *2mm tile spacers* for creating the grout gaps.

The adhesive should be applied with a *notched spreader* (often included), and epoxy grout with a *plastic applicator* or old credit card. Buy some special *cleaning fluid* for wiping off excess grout.

WHERE TO START

Plan the tile layout first, so that any cuts that have to be made are kept to the back of the worktop. You also want to avoid narrow slivers of tile around an inset sink or hob.

If necessary, lay out the tiles in a dry run to check, allowing for a joint spacing of 2mm (any wider is undesirable on a worktop unless the tile edges are uneven, in which case open up the spacing as much as you need to). Whatever the shape of the worktop, you'll find that one 'key' tile influences the position of all the others. Leave this in place as a guide, or mark around it in pencil.

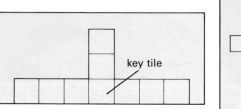

On a plain worktop, plan the layout so that any cuts are kept to the back, and are symmetrical at the sides.

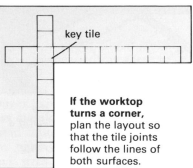

If the worktop turns a corner, plan the layout so that the tile joints follow the lines of both surfaces.

LAYING WHOLE TILES

Where and how you start depends on the design. If you are using edge tiles as the trim, fit these first, then work towards the back of the worktop and any cut-outs. If the edge is being finished with wood trim, pin a batten temporarily along the edge of the worktop as a fixing guide, then work back from here.

When laying the tiles, check regularly with a spirit level that they are all flat. If any stand proud or sit below the surface, don't try to force them; dig them up with an old kitchen knife, adjust the amount of adhesive, and re-lay.

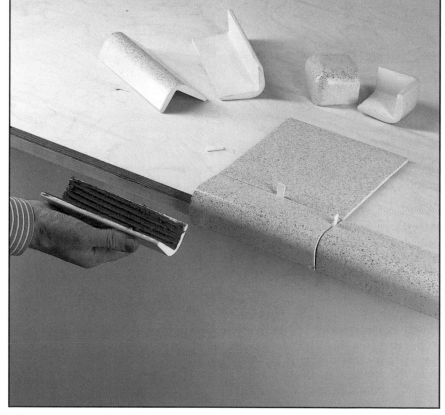

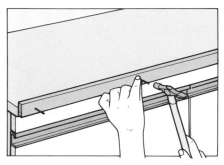

For a wood-trimmed worktop, pin a length of batten along the edge of the worktop as a fixing guide. Don't use the actual trim, as it will be messed up.

For a ceramic edged worktop, start by fixing the edge tiles, using the position of your 'key' tile as a fixing guide. Spread the adhesive on the tile – not the worktop – and check frequently to make sure that the tiles are level.

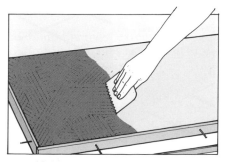

1 *Using a notched spreader, spread enough adhesive to lay 4–5 tiles. The thickness of the adhesive bed should be no more than 2–3mm (⅛").*

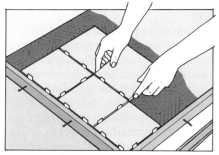

2 Lay the whole tiles in place, with spacers in between. If using a guide batten, fit spacers along this too as the joint with the trim must be grouted.

3 Every 4–5 tiles, use a piece of batten to press the tiles flat, then check them for level against the others. Don't force tiles down – lift and relay.

PLANNING CONSIDERATIONS

As with other forms of rigid tile, the surface to be tiled should be smooth, sound and not liable to move. However, it needn't necessarily be flat – mosaic panels can easily be 'bent' around curves, though if these are too sharp the grout lines open up too far and look unsightly.

One of the major advantages of mosaic tiles is that because of their small size you can usually avoid cutting the tiles themselves. Make this the keynote of your planning and setting out, since it is in any case a fiddly job.

In practice, the smaller the tiles, the more room for manoeuvre you have. This may well influence your choice if you want to tile an awkwardly shaped area, or one full of obstructions such as pipes and electrical sockets.

FLOOR TILING

Mark or chalk a guideline parallel to the most dominant visual feature in the room. (If there isn't one, draw the line to pass through the centre – and square to – the main doorway.) Then lay out the panels in a cross to see how the edge gaps fall.

By carefully juggling the panel positions, you should be able to avoid cutting individual tiles in most places. At this stage mark guidelines at right angles to one another in one corner of the room, three or four tile widths in from the wall.

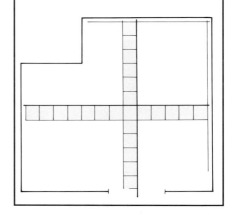

WALL TILING

Contrary to popular opinion, mosaic panels are not fixed from the bottom like ordinary tiles – they are 'hung' like wallpaper, working from the top of the wall, so that the force of gravity keeps the joint spacings even. **Check the top of the wall** (or wherever you are tiling from) with a spirit level.

■ If it is more or less even, you can fix the first panels straight against it.

■ If it is uneven, use a spirit level and long wood straightedge to mark a horizontal start line just over three or four tile widths further down. You can then cut strips of tiles to fit the remaining space and hide any gaps with cornice or wooden moulding.

Check across the wall to see if you can avoid cutting individual tiles at the edges. The easiest way is to cut a batten to the width of a panel, plus an allowance for the joint spacings, then mark off the panel widths on the wall and see how they fall.

If you find yourself left with a wide gap – say, half a tile – adjust the panel positions so that this is distributed evenly between the two sides. The gaps can then be disguised with trim, moulding, or extra grout.

When you've fixed the panel positions, plumb a vertical start line to guide you.

Check the bottom of the wall in the same way, then if necessary redraw the horizontal start line to even up the gaps. Don't worry about a very small gap – it will either be hidden by the floorcovering, or you can disguise it yourself with moulding.

WORKTOP TILING

Mosaic tiles on a worktop must be epoxy-grouted – a very fiddly job. For this reason, you may prefer to confine them to a small area.

If you're starting from scratch, plan the worktop to fit an exact number of tiles. Otherwise, aim to avoid cutting individual tiles by leaving any gap at the back and then covering it with upstand tiles, quadrant tiles, or wooden moulding.

Fitting the tiles around hobs and worktops shouldn't present any problems, since their lips ought to be wide enough to cover any gaps.

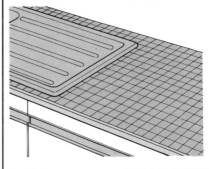

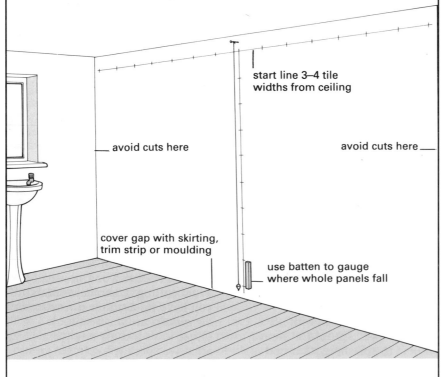

start line 3–4 tile widths from ceiling

avoid cuts here

avoid cuts here

cover gap with skirting, trim strip or moulding

use batten to gauge where whole panels fall

Where wall edges are not straight use horizontal and vertical setting out lines as a guide to fixing panels.

FIXING WALL MOSAICS

1 Apply enough adhesive to the wall to cover about two panels, using a notched spreader. Take care not to obscure the setting-out lines.

2 Press the first panel into place against the setting out lines. Work down and outwards from here, using pieces of card to maintain the joint spacings.

3 After fixing four panels, tap lightly across the surface using a scrap of carpet and a wooden mallet or block of wood as shown. This has the effect of stretching the backing mesh, and ensures that each tile is well bedded in the adhesive.

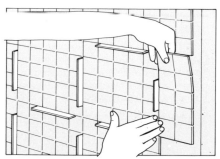

4 Having laid all the whole panels, measure and cut panels to fill in the border areas. Cut through the mesh with a trimming knife, then fit the strips.

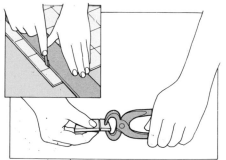

5 Finally, fill any gaps which can't be disguised with pieces of cut tile. To cut, score across the face of the tile with the cutter, then snap with pincers.

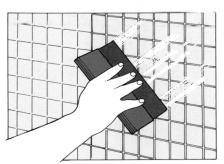

6 Grout the tiles in the usual way, working the grout into the joints with a squeegee, then cleaning off with a sponge. You shouldn't need to 'rub' joints.

PAPER FACED TILES

Some people recommend that paper faced panels are grouted and left to dry before fixing. This stops the adhesive filling up the joints, and produces very smooth, even grout lines, but is impractical if the surface is not completely flat. If you decide to grout conventionally, clear any surplus adhesive that has squeezed through the joints with a small screwdriver after removing the facing. Otherwise, follow the same procedure as for mesh backed panels.

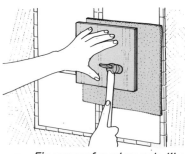

1 Fix paper faced panels like mesh backed ones, starting with whole panels then filling in the edges. Tap over the surface to bed in the tiles.

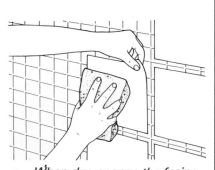

2 When dry, sponge the facing paper with warm water and peel away. Clear any surplus adhesive from the joints, then grout in the usual way.

FLOOR AND WORKTOP TILING

Laying mosaic panels on floors and worktops is much the same as fixing to walls. But since you need to use a thin-bed floor adhesive you should take care not to apply this too thickly or it will squeeze up through the joints and make them impossible to grout. In both cases, don't forget to tap down the tiles with a mallet and strip of carpet every two or three panels, to ensure they are well bedded in.

On a floor there is a risk of the adhesive obscuring the marked lines in the corner of the room, so tack battens along them to guide you. Make sure the battens are at right angles before you begin laying.

Work back towards the door, laying whole panels, then leave to dry for 12 hours before going back and filling in the edge strips. Grout in the usual way.

On a worktop, work towards the back from a guide batten tacked along the front edge. You should be able to prop fittings such as an oven or hob temporarily (see Tip) without having to disconnect them.

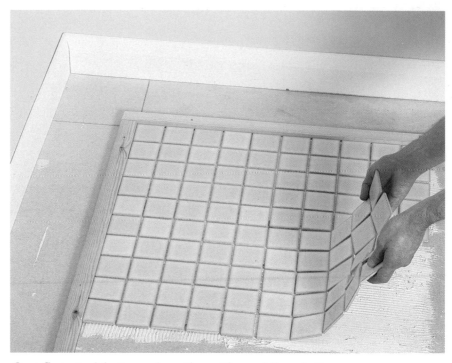

On a floor, tack battens along the setting out lines in the corner of the room, and lay the first panels against these. Work back towards the main door laying whole panels and leave to dry. Then remove the battens and fill in the edge strips.

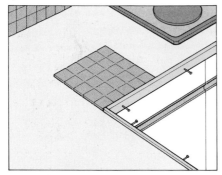

On a worktop, tack a guide batten to the front edge, then lay the panels working towards the back. Start at a point which avoids fiddly cutting at the sides.

After fitting the panels, grout between the joints using two-part epoxy grout. Work on small areas at a time, scraping off the excess as you go.

Trade tip

Around fittings. . .

❝ Around fittings such as a hob or sink, loosen the clip fixings and prop it above the worktop with pieces of wood. Tile two opposite sides and leave to dry, then transfer the wooden props and complete the job. ❞

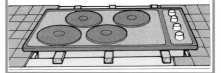

■ PROBLEM SOLVER

Finishing edges and gaps

Depending on the situation, there are several ways to hide the unglazed edges of the panels, or cover gaps to avoid cutting individual tiles.

Hardwood moulding can be pinned and glued to an adjoining surface (eg a worktop edge) or stuck to the tiles with impact adhesive.

Alternatively, use *quadrant tiles* or *plain tiles*, stuck to the mosaics with tile adhesive.

Plastic trim strips bedded in the tile adhesive before laying are ideal for finishing corners and other exposed edges.

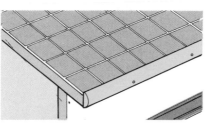
hardwood edge moulding (pinned)

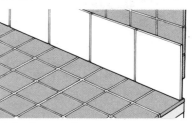
plain tiles used to cover gaps

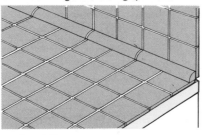
quadrant tiles

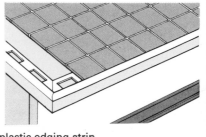
plastic edging strip

LAYING CERAMIC AND QUARRY TILES

Of all the readily available coverings for floors, ceramic and quarry tiles are the longest-lived and hardest wearing. Laid properly, a hard-tiled floor should add substantially to the value of your home, and the huge range of styles available leaves plenty of scope for expressing your own personal taste.

Before going ahead, however, it's as well to consider the limitations:

■ Most hard tiles raise the level of the floor substantially, which could involve removing skirtings, trimming doors, and fitting wooden ramps with adjoining floor surfaces.

■ Hard tiles are as good as permanent, so you should think twice before laying them around built-ins – for example, kitchen units; the chances are the units will be the first to go, leaving holes that you may not be able to match.

■ Solid floors are better suited to hard tiling than suspended wooden ones. It is *possible* to tile a wooden floor, but only if it is absolutely free of structural movement, and properly lined with plywood. Remember, too, that you won't have access to services running under the floor once the tiles are firmly fixed in place.

Ceramic tiles (left) and quarry tiles (below) are hardwearing and practical in halls and kitchens.

PRELIMINARY WORK

Aim to get as much preliminary work as possible done before buying the tiles (see overleaf).

■ Skirtings should ideally be removed so that they can be refitted to hide the cut tiles around the edge of the floor. However, this may be more trouble than it's worth if the skirtings are the deep ornate type.

■ Remove as much built-in furniture as you can. Again, ideally, the tiles should run from wall to wall.

■ Line a wooden boarded floor with exterior grade plywood.

■ On a solid floor, check the level: a *thick-bed adhesive* (see overleaf) will accommodate variations of up to about 12mm (½″) but for anything greater, fill hollows then resurface with self-smoothing compound.

■ Remove inward-opening doors ready for trimming later.

■ Nail battens temporarily across doorways to give yourself something to tile against.

Prise off skirtings with a bolster or crowbar, using a block of wood to protect the plaster.

Line a boarded floor with sheets of 12mm (½″) plywood, staggering the joints.

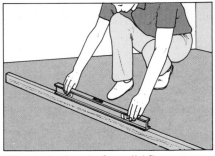

Check the level of a solid floor at various points. If it varies by over 12mm (½″), resurface.

Temporarily nail battens across doors to provide an edge for tiling against.

CHOOSING AND BUYING THE TILES

DIY shops, builders' merchants and superstores stock limited runs of the more popular ranges of ceramic floor tile, but their choice of quarries is generally limited. For the widest selection of all types, visit a tile supplier: most have panels showing the finished effect, which may not be as you imagined.

Floor tiles are normally sold by the square metre or square yard, so make sure you're armed with the room dimensions and add 8–10% extra for wastage depending on how much cutting you anticipate.

Wherever you buy the tiles, the same outlet will also be able to supply the adhesive, grout, and any special tools (see opposite).

Ceramic tiles

Ceramic floor tiles are thicker than wall tiles – most are at least 6mm (1/4") – but have the same glazed finish. The majority are machine-made; hand-made floor tiles are harder to lay and often expensive.

Many floor tile patterns look identical to wall tiles, so be sure to specify 'floor tiles' when ordering. Others imitate materials such as stone flags, marble or granite. And as well as a choice of colour and pattern style, you are likely to come across a variety of surface finishes – for example, matt or gloss, smooth or textured.

Popular square and rectangular sizes are 150×100mm, 150×150mm, 200×150mm and 200×200mm (about 6×4, 6×6, 8×6 and 8×8"). There are also hexagonal and interlocking shapes.

Decorative insets for ceramic floor tiles are often sold as part of a range. But whereas wall insets are usually tile-sized (or multiple tile-sized) motifs, floor insets tend to take the form of much smaller decorative tiles which you interlock with the main tiles or 'build in' at the corner joints.

Quarry tiles

Unglazed quarry tiled floors have enjoyed a revival over the past few years, and their warm, natural tones are well suited to more rustic decorative schemes. Even so, the subtle colour ranges, plus the chance to use contrasting ceramic insets, can create exciting effects.

Quarries are sold in the same way as ceramics, and come in similar sizes and shapes, but they are much thicker – from around 10mm (3/8") to as much as 25mm (1"). They are also never uniform in size, which is part of their appeal.

When choosing quarries, always ask to see a finished panel so that you can gauge the effect.

Adhesives and grout

Ceramic tiles are generally laid using a *thin-bed adhesive*, spread to a thickness of around 3mm (1/8"). This comes ready mixed in tubs of various sizes, or slightly more cheaply in powder form for mixing with water; one type has a latex additive and is designed specially for wooden floors. Coverage is about 2.5litres (1/2 gal) per sq m (1.2sq yd) for ready mixed; 2.75kg (6lb) per sq m for powder.

For thicker ceramic tiles and all quarry tiles, use a *thick-bed adhesive*. This is spread up to 12mm (1/2") thick, and so is capable of taking up the natural variations in the thickness of the tiles. (Professionals usually lay quarries in a sand and cement screed, but this is a lot harder than it looks and is not recommended for DIY.)

Thick-bed adhesive comes in powder form and looks like cement (on which it is based). Coverage is around 11kg (24lb) per sq m (1.2sq yd), but always order on the generous side.

Grout for floor tiles is generally sold in powder form. There is a range of colours for ceramics, plus more natural looking cement-based types for quarries. Coverage depends on the thickness of the tiles and on how wide you decide to make the joints – ask your supplier's advice.

For quarry tiles, you also need a means of sealing the unglazed surface. Most professionals favour 2–3 coats of *boiled linseed oil* thinned with 50% white spirit. One litre of the mixture covers about 20sq m.

Practical ideas include diagonal tiling in narrow rooms (below) and non-slip finishes (left).

DESIGN CHECKLIST – QUARRIES
■ Could the floor do with rescreeding? In this case you'd be better getting a professional to lay the tiles the traditional way in a mortar bed.
■ Does the room in question open out on to a small patio or yard? If funds permit, you could consider quarry tiling this too.
■ Do you want to refit the skirtings? Some quarry tile ranges include skirting tiles (with special tiles for internal and external corners), but you'll need to allow for these when setting out the tiling (see overleaf).
■ For a high-gloss finish, ask your supplier about special sealants and lacquers.

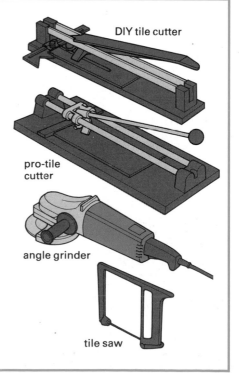

When choosing quarry tiles for a kitchen, a glazed or sealed finish is more practical (left). Larger tiles may help to give a feeling of space (above).

.... Shopping List ....

As well as the tiles and adhesive, you'll need a complete set of tiling tools.

A notched spreader for applying the adhesive; the plasterer's trowel pattern is best for floors.

A tile cutter – see Tip.

A tile file for finishing the edges of cut tiles.

A spirit level and wood or metal straightedge for keeping a check on the floor level.

A try square, chalk lines and tape for squaring things up.

Softwood battens for setting out – 50×25mm (2×1″) is a useful size. You also need a hammer and nails to fix them.

A bucket and stirring implement (an old slotted spoon is ideal) for mixing the adhesive and grout.

A rubber squeegee and sponge for applying the grout, plus a wooden dowel for finishing the joints.

Trade tip

Cutting floor tiles

❝ Even the thinner floor tiles are much harder to cut than wall tiles, and an ordinary wall tile cutter won't do. Alternatives are:
■ A lightweight floor tile cutter – reasonably cheap to buy, and suitable for most ceramic tiles up to around 6mm (¼″) thick.
■ A professional tile cutter – available for hire from most hire shops, or where you buy the tiles. This copes easily with ceramic tiles and with thinner quarries.
■ An angle grinder – easily hired – is the best tool for cutting thick quarries, and is useful for 'nibbling' awkward shapes. You also need full protective gear – goggles, gloves and a mask.

  If you're not using an angle grinder, a tile saw is the best tool for cutting out small pieces. ❞

DIY tile cutter

pro-tile cutter

angle grinder

tile saw

SETTING OUT

As with all floor tiles, the first stage is to set out the tiling so that you avoid awkward cuts and narrow gaps around the edges of the room. The procedure is basically the same for both ceramics and quarries, but differs slightly from that used for other types of floor tile.

Start by snapping chalked string lines to cross at right angles to one another in the centre of the room. The first chalk line represents the 'line' of the tile joints as seen from the main doorway: it must run parallel to the dominant visual line in the room – the longest wall, the bath, or a run of kitchen units – otherwise the tiles will appear 'crooked' as you walk into the room.

If you have difficulty deciding on a dominant feature, draw the line from the centre – and at right angles to – the main doorway.

After snapping the second line, measure off in whole tiles along the arms of the cross to see what sort of gaps are left at the edges. You can do this by laying out the tiles themselves (not forgetting to allow the correct joint gap – see below), but it's easier to make up a tiling gauge (see Tip).

Ideally, no edge gap should be less than a third of a tile's width. If your measuring reveals otherwise, shift the position of one or both lines so that the gaps are evened up and then try again.

Fixing setting out battens

When you are happy with the positions of the lines, decide in which quadrant to begin tiling, bearing in mind that you'll be starting in one corner and working back towards the door. Use your tiling gauge to mark the positions of the last whole tiles in the quadrant, then join the marks into guidelines using a straightedge.

Next, cut two battens roughly to the length of the guidelines. Nail them along the lines as shown, so that they sit on the 'gap' side, not the 'whole tile' side. Use a carpenter's try square to check that the battens are at 90°. You are then ready to start laying the tiles.

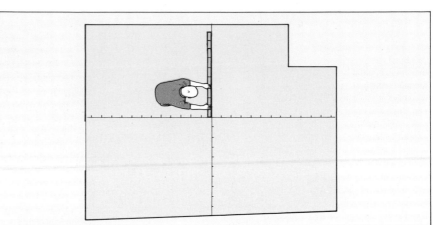

Setting out stage 1: chalk lines across the room to align with the dominant visual feature, then use your tile gauge to find out how the gaps fall at the edges.

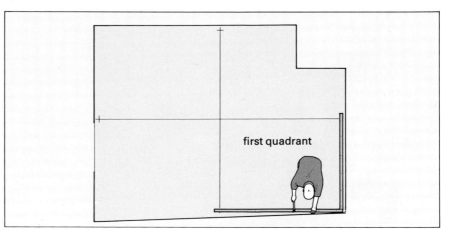

Setting out stage 2: having adjusted the chalk lines as necessary, draw guidelines around the edge of the first quadrant to be tiled and nail battens against them.

WHAT JOINT SPACING?

Unlike many wall tiles, floor tiles are always square edged and must be laid with an allowance for the joint spacing. Nor are there any hard and fast rules as to how wide the spacing should be; much depends on the tile, and on the sort of look you want – the wider the joints, the more obviously 'tiled' the finished effect becomes.

As a general rule, for ceramics the spacing should be narrow – between 2 and 4mm ($1/16$–$1/8$). For quarries, which don't have straight edges, it must necessarily be wider – approximately 4–10mm ($1/8$–$3/8''$).

Unless you've seen finished samples of the tiling, it's worth experimenting before you start setting out. When you've decided on the spacing, find something to use as a gauge – a piece of thick card, a thin wall tile or a slip of plywood are all popular choices.

Trade tip

Make a gauge

❝ A tiling gauge makes it easy to measure off whole tile widths with an allowance for the joints.

For ceramics, simply mark off tile widths and joint spacings along a straight batten.

For quarries, where neither the tiles nor the gaps are a consistent width, pick 8–10 tiles at random and lay them out in a row. Adjust the joints until they look more or less even, then mark off. ❞

LAYING CERAMICS

The basic laying procedure for ceramics is to start tiling against the setting out battens, then continue laying whole tiles back towards the door. With all the whole tiles laid, leave the adhesive to set for at least 12 hours. Then remove the setting out battens and cut and lay the edge tiles.

Spread the adhesive in batches roughly a metre square. Use the spacing tool to make sure that each tile sits square to its neighbours.

Check regularly that the tiles sit level. In particular, make sure that the tiles on one patch of adhesive are level with those on the next, as this is where problems usually occur. If you find that the level is 'out', lift the tiles immediately and re-trowel the adhesive bed to bring it to the correct thickness.

When it comes to fitting the edge tiles, mark them individually using a whole tile to gauge the profile of the wall. For straight cuts use the tile cutter; see Problem Solver for how to deal with awkward shapes.

When laying the edge tiles, spread the adhesive on the backs of the tiles, and spread it slightly more thickly than you did on the floor.

1 Using a notched spreader, spread a 1m (1.1yd) square layer of adhesive in the corner formed by the battens. Thickness of the bed should be around 3mm (⅛″).

2 Slide the first tile into the corner and press down gently. (Note that if adhesive squeezes up over the edges you are pressing too hard.)

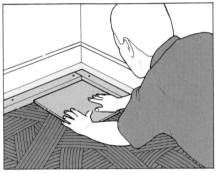

3 Position the next tile, using your spacing gauge to ensure it sits square to the first. Continue in this way until the adhesive area is filled.

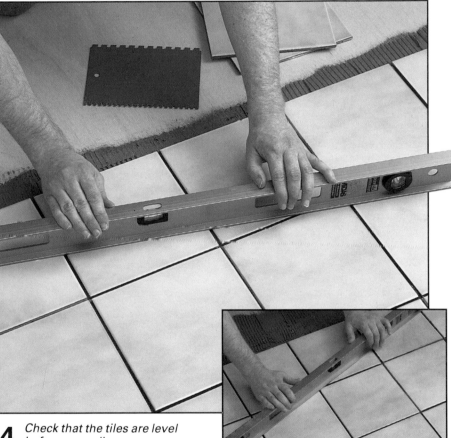

4 Check that the tiles are level before spreading more adhesive. Check again (inset) after laying the next few tiles in case the two areas don't match.

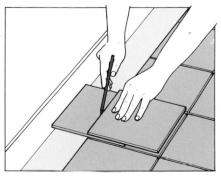

5 Having laid all the whole tiles and allowed the adhesive to dry, mark the edge tiles individually to fit using a whole tile to gauge the wall profile.

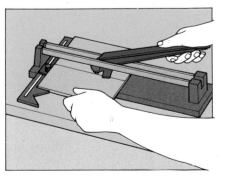

6 To make straight cuts, lay the tile face up in the cutting jig. Score down the marked line, then depress the lever – the tile should snap cleanly.

7 Apply adhesive to the backs of the cut tiles with the notched spreader and position them with the cut edge against the wall. Press gently into place.

LAYING QUARRIES

Quarry tiles stuck with thick-bed adhesive (as opposed to mortar) are laid in virtually the same way as ceramic tiles. The main difference is that the thickness of the adhesive (and the unevenness of some quarries) makes it slightly more difficult to keep everything level.

■ Mix and spread the adhesive in 1m (1.1yd) square batches to a depth of around 10mm (⅜″).

■ Set the tiles in place using only very light pressure – don't worry about levelling them.

■ When the patch of adhesive is covered, use a sturdy wood block to press the tiles down level with one another; avoid putting pressure on any one tile in particular.

Repeat this sequence for all the whole tiles, then leave to dry before fitting the edge tiles.

Set quarry tiles in place with very light pressure, spacing the joints as evenly as you can. After covering each spread batch of adhesive, use a stout block of wood to tap the tiles down level with one another.

GROUTING AND FINISHING

Both ceramics and quarries are grouted in the same way as wall tiles – preferably at least 12 hours after fitting the edge tiles.

Mix up the grout in a bucket according to the maker's instructions and stir thoroughly to remove lumps. Use immediately and work fast – it doesn't take long for it to become unworkable. Make sure, too, that you remove the excess grout from the face of the tiles before it dries; quarries in particular are susceptible to staining, since they are unglazed.

Sealing quarry tiles is best done before you grout, to protect the surface from staining, but take your supplier's advice. Apply two coats of thinned linseed oil with a clean cloth and leave to dry overnight.

1 Mix up the grout according to the instructions and spread it over the tiles. Work it into the joints using a rubber squeegee, then sponge up the excess.

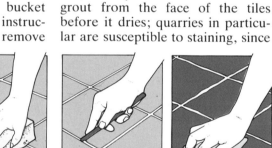

2 Check that there are no air pockets, then leave the joints until just hard. Finish with a piece of dowel (ceramics) or rub with a coarse cloth (quarries).

Trade tip

Cleaning off

6 The best way to clean grout stains off floor tiles is with sawdust. Spread it over the floor and rub with a damp cloth, then just sweep up the residue. 9

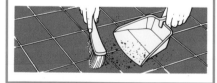

▮ PROBLEM SOLVER ▮

Cutting awkward shapes

Don't be too ambitious when cutting edge tiles to fit tricky shapes such as architraves or pipes – stick to simple, straight cuts (if you try to notch tiles, they'll break), then rely on the grout to fill any gaps.

Ceramics are best cut clamped in a workbench using a tile saw. For quarries, use an angle grinder; work outside, wear full protective gear and take great care – especially to avoid cutting the lead.

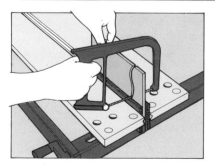

Awkward shapes are best marked by measuring direct. Most ceramic floor tiles can be cut with a tile saw; clamp them in a bench with protective padding.

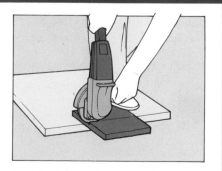

Thick tiles such as quarries are best cut with an angle grinder – wear stout boots and support the tile as shown. Don't put down the grinder until the wheel stops.

LAYING CORK FLOOR TILES

Cork tiling is a warm, resilient and very economical floorcovering. The tiles are light and relatively easy to handle, and the pre-sealed types require little finishing work.

Choosing tiles

Most cork tiles are 12″ (305mm) square, and are sold in packs of nine to cover 1 sq yd (just under 1 sq m). Although they are available in different grades to suit different levels of wear, the main choice is between *sealed* and *unsealed* – some have a protective coat of acrylic varnish, lacquer or PVC applied in the factory, while others are sanded but left 'raw'. You can also get cork tiles with a self-adhesive backing, in which case they can be treated like self-adhesive vinyl tiles.

Sealed tiles are ready to walk on as soon as they are laid, but the square-edged type must be closely butted together or there is a risk of water seeping down between the joints. Some better quality tiles have lipped edges which interlock to seal the joints.

Unsealed tiles must be sealed before taking any foot traffic. The normal method is to give them at least three coats of polyurethane varnish, allowing each coat to dry thoroughly before applying the next, so it could take several days before the floor is ready for use.

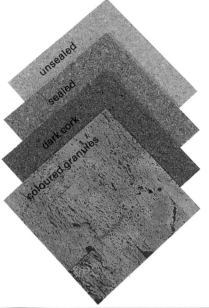

unsealed

sealed

dark cork

coloured granules

.... Shopping List ....

Most manufacturers provide charts on their packaging indicating how many tiles you need for a given area allowing for wastage. But to make use of this information, you must first measure the floor.

In a regularly shaped room, simply multiply the length by the width. In a room full of awkward shapes it's safer to draw a sketch plan and divide the area into a number of rectangles; find the area of each one, then add them together to get the total area.

Adhesive choice is critical, and will make all the difference to the durability of the floor. In theory, most water-based PVA flooring adhesives are suitable, but recent research suggests that some brands cause certain types of cork to expand and contract as they dry out, leading to shrinkage and gaps.

The problem is less acute on unsealed tiles, where the adhesive can evaporate more easily, and on vinyl-backed tiles, where it doesn't come into contact with the cork. But in all cases, follow the maker's recommendations where given.

Coverage depends on the porosity of the subfloor and on the tiles. As a rough guide, 1 litre will cover around 3–4 sq m (4 sq yd) on a concrete screed – more if the floor is lined with hardboard or the tiles have a smooth backing.

Sealant is usually gloss polyurethane varnish, but again you should follow the manufacturer's own recommendations. You need at least three coats, but on a floor taking heavy wear it's worth applying an extra one for good measure.

One litre of polyurethane covers about 16 sq m (19 sq yd) per coat, but allow for the fact that the first coat should be thinned half and half with white spirit to help it soak into the cork.

Tools checklist: Adhesive spreader (often supplied), string and chalk, tape measure, try square, trimming knife and spare blades, steel wool, wall brush (for applying sealant).

Trade tip

Matt finish

❝ If you want a satin or matt finish on cork tiles which you plan to seal yourself, apply a couple of gloss coats first – it is much tougher. You can then use your chosen varnish for the top couple of coats to give a more subdued effect. ❞

FLOOR PREPARATION

The first step is to prepare the underlying floor surface.

Boarded floors need lining with sheets of hardboard. Arrange the sheets so they don't coincide with the joints between boards and nail at 225mm (9") centres (150mm (6") around the edges).

Solid floors must be level, smooth and dry. If the surface is simply dusty, coat with concrete stabilizer. Localized damage can be repaired with concrete floor repair compound.

If the floor is slightly uneven, heavily patched or covered with small lumps and bumps, resurface it with self-levelling compound. But if the level is badly 'out' – over 12mm (½") say – or there are signs of dampness, have it rescreeded.

Existing floorcoverings may provide a suitable surface – for example, old cork tiles, vinyl tiles or glued-down sheet vinyl can all be overlaid with cork tiles, as long as they are level and

firmly fixed. Ceramic tiles may be more of a problem if the joints are deeply indented (though you cold consider filling them). Old quarry tiled floors need treating with caution, as they may have been laid without a damp-proof membrane underneath. It's safer to lift them and rescreed.

Always check the adhesive manufacturer's instructions – they may recommend priming or sealing a particular surface to ensure a good bond.

DECIDING WHERE TO START

Few rooms have walls which are exactly square to one another, and even fewer are the right size to take a whole number of tiles. So the standard procedure for laying floor tiles is to start from a point near the centre of the floor, and work out towards the edges.

The exact starting point depends on how the gaps fall around the edges. By laying out the tiles in a 'dry run' as shown below, you can adjust it so that the gaps are more or less even right around the room, with no unsightly narrow strips.

Taking a line

If there is a major feature in the room which catches the eye – for example, a run of units – it may be better for the line of the tile joints to run parallel with this, rather than the walls. (Otherwise, the tiles could appear to be askew when in position.)

Arrange for this by making sure that one of the setting-out lines runs parallel to the feature concerned. Then reset the other line at right angles to it.

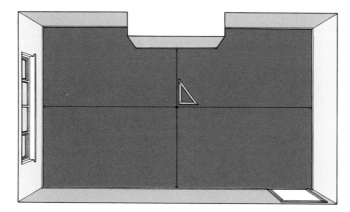

Find the centre of the room by measuring and marking the midpoints of the four walls, then stretching string between them. Check with a try square where the lines cross, and adjust one line until you get a right angle.

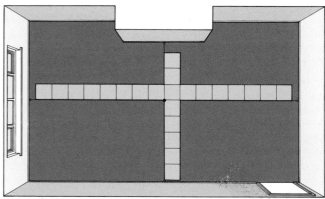

Lay 'dry runs' of tiles out from the centre point towards the walls and see what sort of gaps are formed around edges of the room. Ideally, there should be about half a tile's width all round.

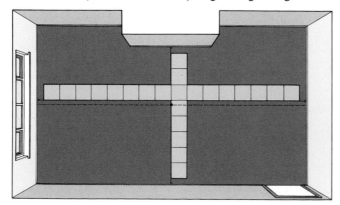

Reposition the centre tile(s) if necessary so that the gaps are evened up – for example, position the first tile over the cross instead of in the angle. If none of the positions is satisfactory, try moving one or both of the string lines.

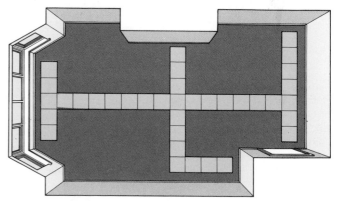

If the room is an awkward shape, lay further dry runs towards each obstacle and check the gaps here. Some awkward cuts will be unavoidable, but try to keep them to unobtrusive areas.

Check the tiles

❛ Before you start laying the tiles, check them carefully for grain pattern and colour. This is easiest while you have them laid out in a dry run.

Some tiles have very definite markings, with chips of cork aligned in rows. If a grain like this is laid running the same way right across the floor, it makes the tiles less obvious; conversely, alternating the grain direction actually strengthens the tiled effect. Decide which you prefer and lay the tiles accordingly.

At the same time, check for colour variation between packs. Unlike wallpaper, cork tiles aren't produced in batch numbers since some colour variation occurs naturally. Even so, you can avoid blocks of lighter or darker tiles by mixing the packs and then laying different tones at random. ❜

When laying cork tiles use a recommended adhesive. Spread the adhesive on the subfloor then position the tiles.

LAYING WHOLE TILES

Once you have decided on your starting point, adjust the strings to align with the central tile(s), then cover them with chalk and snap them against the floor to mark two straight guidelines.

Lay the tiles in a pyramid shape, working from the centre of the room to the wall furthest from the door. Fill in the corners with whole tiles, then work back towards the door in the same way.

When all the whole tiles are in position, leave the adhesive to set for 24 hours before filling in gaps. This way, there's no danger of them becoming dislodged.

1 Starting from the marked point, use a notched spreader to apply enough adhesive to lay about nine tiles. Work towards the wall furthest from the door.

2 Lay two or three tiles along one line, then start outwards along the intersecting line. Fill in the angle, butting to two edges where possible.

3 Use a clean cloth to wipe off any adhesive which squeezes out of the joints on to the tile surface. Moisten the rag with white spirit if necessary.

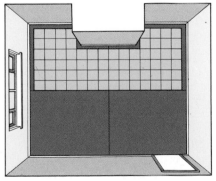

4 Work out from the centre line until half the room is covered. Then repeat for the second half, until all the whole tiles are laid.

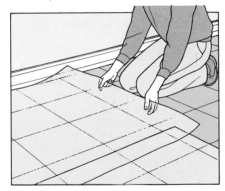

5 If you are using unsealed tiles, protect them by laying sheets of polythene over the surface of the tiles. Leave until the next day before sealing.

FILLING IN THE EDGES

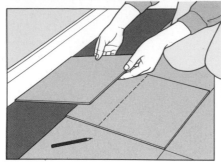

1 Lay the tile to be cut over the last complete tile, aligning the edges exactly. Position an uncut tile on top, so one edge butts against the wall.

2 Using the top tile as a guide, mark a cutting line on the tile to be cut. Then lay the tile on a hard surface and trim along the marked line with a trimming knife.

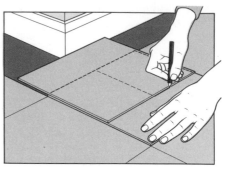

3 At external angles, use the same technique twice to mark both cutting lines. If you are using unsealed tiles, be careful not to mark beyond the angle.

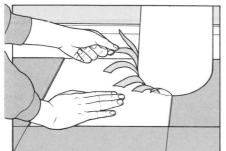

4 For rounded shapes like a basin pedestal, use a paper template. Tear back the paper so it fits round the obstacle, then use it to mark the tile.

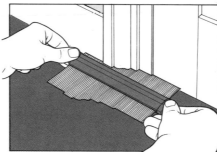

5 For fiddly obstacles, such as the ornate architrave around a doorway, use a profile gauge to trace the exact shape then cut it out a notch at a time.

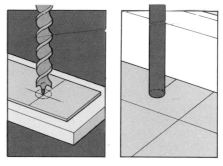

6 Around pipes, trim the tile to fit the gap, then measure the position of the pipe and cut or drill a suitable hole. Finally, slit the tile and slide in place.

SEALING THE TILES

Unsealed tiles have to be coated to protect the surface from everyday wear and tear. Cork in its natural state is highly absorbent, leaving it vulnerable to grease marks and water penetration (which could cause the tiles to lift).

If there is any unevenness in the surface (there shouldn't be if the floor has been properly prepared), sand down with medium glasspaper. Before you start, vacuum the floor thoroughly, and wipe over to remove all traces of dust (see Tip).

Trade tip

Dealing with dust

❛ To ensure a dust- and grease-free surface before and during sealing, wipe down the tiles with a clean, white lint-free cloth moistened with white spirit. Keep the rag just moist enough to pick up the dust without wetting the tiles. The same trick can be used for other wooden surfaces before painting or varnishing – white spirit doesn't raise the grain the way water would. ❜

Apply at least three coats of polyurethane varnish to unsealed tiles. Rub down with a pad of fine steel wool and wipe off the dust after each coat.

LAYING
CARPET TILES

Carpet tiles are one of the most economical forms of 'soft' flooring. As well as being easy to lay – much easier, for instance, than broad-loom carpet – their toughness and washability make them the ideal choice for a floor that's going to take heavy wear.

Choosing carpet tiles

Once you've decided on carpet tiles, it's worth taking a good look at the selection available. Large department stores and specialist flooring shops tend to stock more extensive ranges than DIY super-stores.

Some tiles – designed for commercial use – are extra-heavy duty, with a coarse pile that's none too soft to the touch. Other heavy-duty tiles have an almost felt-like texture, with an easy-clean short pile that usually incorporates a simple, geometric pattern.

For home use, tiles which imitate popular carpet styles are likely to be a better choice. There are plenty to choose from, including Berber and other looped pile styles, as well as softer piles for bedrooms and special deep-pile styles for bathrooms. Before deciding, see *Deciding on a pattern* overleaf.

Special qualities

Most carpet tiles are washable. They are usually laid without adhesive (and never stuck permanently) so you can lift them for cleaning and drying – or in some cases, even wash them under a tap.

Construction varies slightly from make to make, but all carpet tiles (unlike most other forms of carpet) have a highly stable backing which won't shrink, stretch or distort.

Carpet tiles – tough, practical and easy to lay.

Even so, you should check on suitability for a particular situation before buying; some carpet tiles, for example, are unsuitable for areas where they may get damp, such as kitchens and bathrooms. Nor can you lay carpet tiles on stairs – at least, not without going to a great deal of trouble.

....Shopping List....

Carpet tiles are sold in squares measuring 400mm (15¾") or 500mm (19½"). the ready-reckoner charts on the right show how many whole tiles of each size are needed to fill various sized rooms, allowing for wastage. Other ways of calculating coverage may be given on the tile packaging.

Like wallpaper, carpet tiles are made in numbered batches. Make sure the packs all have the same batch number, and don't be tempted to skimp – you may not be able to match them if you have to buy more later.

Adhesive is usually optional, depending largely on the smoothness of the existing floor surface. On a slippery surface it may be helpful to glue the first four tiles and then every tenth one (see overleaf) to guard against 'creeping' in the future. Special low-tack *carpet tile adhesive* is available for this in aerosol form. Alternatively, use a latex-based adhesive such as Copydex.

Tools checklist: The only specialist tool you need is a stretcher for butting tiles tightly against each other. There's no need to hire a proper knee kicker – make your own hand-held stretcher from a wood offcut and a few nails as described on sheet 38. Other tools include a tape measure, string, chalk, metal rule or straight edge, and a trimming knife.

Using 400mm (15¾") square tiles:

Length	Room width				
	1m (3')	2m (6')	3m (9')	4m (12')	5m (15')
1m (3')	9	15	24	30	39
2m (6')	15	25	40	50	65
3m (9')	24	40	64	80	104
4m (12')	30	50	80	100	130
5m (15')	39	65	104	130	169
6m (18')	45	75	120	150	195

Using 500mm (19½") square tiles

Length	Room width				
	1m (3')	2m (6')	3m (9')	4m (12')	5m (15')
1m (3')	9	15	21	27	33
2m (6')	15	25	35	45	55
3m (9')	21	35	49	63	77
4m (12')	27	45	63	81	99
5m (15')	33	55	77	99	121
6m (18')	39	65	91	117	143

DECIDING ON A PATTERN

Examining your chosen tiles, you may find there is a definite direction to the pile: rub your hand over it one way and it feels smooth (*with the pile*); rub it the other way and it resists (*against* the pile). There may also be an arrow on the back of the tiles indicating the pile direction, as an aid when laying them.

In this case, you have a choice. Laying all the tiles with the pile running in the same direction will disguise the joints and create a smooth, even-coloured effect similar to carpet. On the other hand, if you lay each tile with the pile direction running at right angles to the one before, the result will be a subtle chequerboard effect that's unique to carpet tiles. In a small room, this can be used to create extra visual interest.

(Some manufacturers recommend that you always lay the tiles in a chequerboard pattern even if there is no definite pile; certain makes have ribs on the backs, so this stops them from slipping around.)

Other patterns

Carpet tiles give you the opportunity to create your own patterns – perhaps using different coloured tiles from the same range. In this case, it's worth drawing a scale plan of the room on 5mm squared paper and trying out different designs before you buy.

Preparing the floor

Like cork and vinyl tiles, carpet tiles can go on any smooth, dry surface – new floorboards or chipboard, or a properly levelled concrete floor. On a wood surface, make sure the boards or sheets are firmly fixed, and that all nail heads are punched well below the surface.

Old floorboards full of gaps and bumps need levelling with hardboard. Lay the sheets rough side up, so the tiles have something to grip.

Uneven concrete floors can be filled and resurfaced with self-levelling compound, but check for damp first. Treat with stabilizer if the surface is sound but dusty.

FINDING THE STARTING POINT

As with other tiles, it's best to start from a point roughly in the centre of the room and work outwards along chalked lines snapped at right angles to one corner. The first line determines what feature in the room the tiles are aligned with.

■ If the walls are reasonably square, align with these; measure their midpoints, then mark the floor at corresponding points and snap the chalk line between them.

■ If the walls are out of square, it's better to align the tiles with the most dominant feature – a run of kitchen units, say, or a bath. In this case, find the midpoints of the *adjacent* walls and mark the floor as before. Adjust the marks so that they are equidistant from the feature, then snap the chalk line.

■ If you are unsure what to align with, draw the first line at right angles to the doorway, so you see a straight run as you enter the room.

■ Snap a second line at right angles

to the first near the middle of the room (use a couple of tiles butted closely together to check the angle). Then lay out the tiles in a dry run along each arm of the cross and see what sort of spaces you're left with around the edges.

The aim is to keep the cut tiles more or less the same size all round, and to avoid awkward corners or narrow slivers. If necessary, alter the position of one or both lines to arrange this.

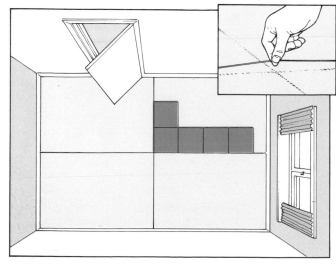

Where walls are square, *snap chalked lines at right angles to each other across the middle of the room. Starting where the lines cross, lay dry runs of tiles along each arm, and see what gaps are left at the edges of the room.*

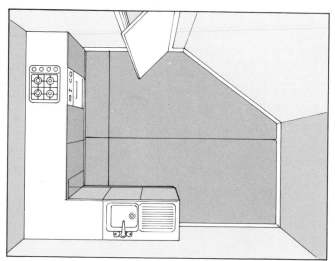

If the walls are not square, *adjust the first line to run parallel with the most dominant feature in the room. Snap a second line at right angles, then lay dry runs of tiles and check the gaps. Adjust the lines if necessary.*

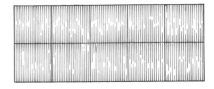

To lay in a chequerboard pattern (left) alternate the direction of the pile (or arrows on backs).

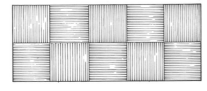

For a broadloom effect (above) position the tiles with the pile (and arrows) running the same way.

LAYING THE TILES

Starting at the intersection of the two chalk lines, lay whole tiles out along each arm of the cross and fit the edge tiles (see overleaf) so that subsequent rows have something to butt up against. If one arm of the cross coincides with a doorway, fix a batten across it temporarily to give you something to butt up to.

Next, fill in the corners of the cross with whole tiles, applying dabs of glue where appropriate. Then fill in the remaining edge tiles.

Trade tip

Making a stretcher

❝ Make a hand-held stretcher from an offcut of board about 300mm (12") square and 18-25mm (¾-1") thick. From one side, screw on a piece of dowel or broom handle; from the other, drive in a series of nails at a slight angle so that their tips protrude about 2mm (¹⁄₁₀").

To use, simply press down on the tile and shove hard. ❞

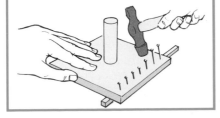

1 Lay whole tiles along each of the marked lines, out towards the edge of the room. Butt them tightly, and alternate the pile direction if required.

3 Fill in the corners of the cross, working out from the centre in a diamond pattern. Use your home-made stretcher to keep the tiles tightly butted.

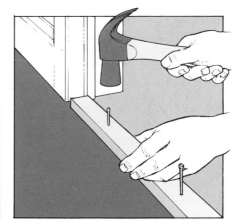

2 Cut tiles to fit the ends of the rows (see overleaf), to leave a tightly butted cross. If necessary, fix a batten across a doorway to butt tiles against.

Where tiles need gluing spray the backs with special adhesive and press into place. Alternatively, spread a blob of latex adhesive in the middle of the backing.

FITTING EDGE TILES

Unlike other types of tile, you need to start cutting tiles almost immediately – as soon as you've completed the four arms of the cross. This keeps the whole tiles locked together and gives you something to butt the others against.

Cut the tiles with a metal straight edge and a sharp trimming knife. You can't mark the tops of the tiles, so measure and mark on the back and remember to reverse the marks when you turn the tile over.

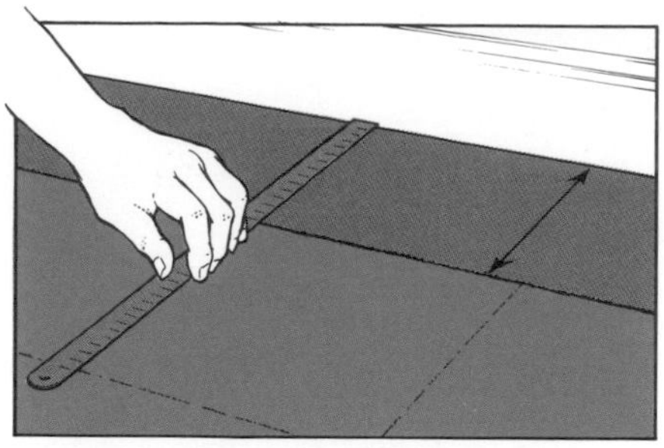

1 *Measure the distance from the last complete tile to the skirting or fitting. Measure from both sides of the tile as the distance may vary.*

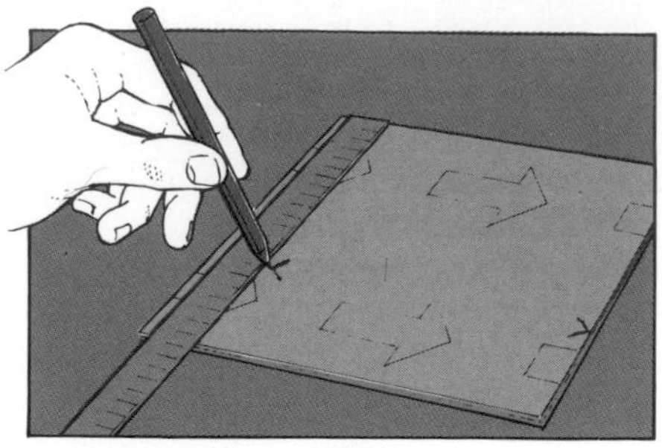

2 *Transfer the measurements to the back of the tile, not forgetting to reverse them. Use V-shaped marks to ensure complete accuracy.*

Trade tip

Wiping the knife

❛ Many carpet tiles have a bituminous layer built into the backing, and this can get on to the blade and stain the pile. To stop this happening, keep a cloth soaked in white spirit handy and get into the habit of wiping the knife blade after each cut. ❜

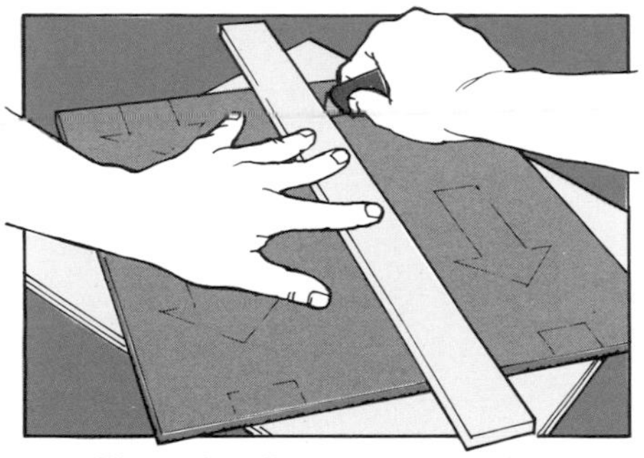

3 *Place the tile on a piece of board or old tile. Align the straight edge with the two marks, hold the tile firmly, and make repeated passes with the knife.*

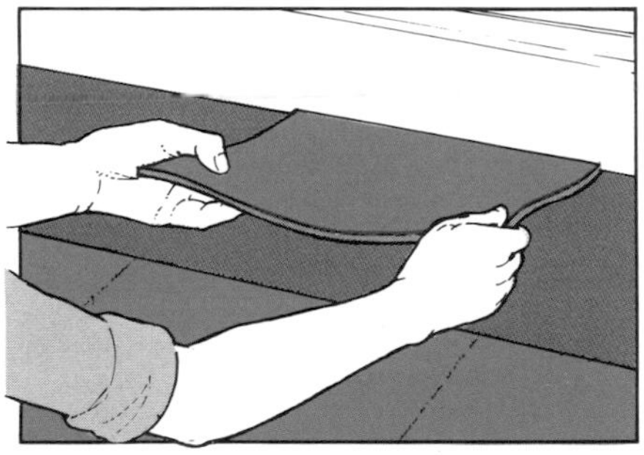

4 *Trim off any stray fibres or slivers of backing and slot the cut tile into place. Make sure the cut edge goes against the skirting or fitting.*

PROBLEM SOLVER

Fitting around obstacles

If you need to make anything other than single straight cuts, use the 'double tile technique'.

■ Position the last whole tile and lay the tile to be cut on top of it, pile uppermost.

■ Take another complete tile and lay it over the space to be filled, butted against the edge.

■ Mark the edge of the tile being cut in felt tip pen, then transfer the marks to the back.

■ On internal or external corners, repeat the process to mark a second cutting line.

Around curved or uneven edges, such as the base of a WC, use a template.

■ Take a piece of stiff paper or light card and cut it to the size of a tile.

■ Lay the template in position, butted to the last whole tiles, and clip in around edge until you can ease it around the obstacle.

■ Use your fingers to mark a crease, then trim the edge of the template and double-check the fit. Mark which side of the template is the top.

■ Place the template wrong side up on the back of the tile and trace the outline. Trim freehand with the knife, scoring repeatedly until you have cut right through.

Around small pipes, it helps if you have an offcut of the same size pipe to use as a template or to make the hole.

■ Start by measuring and cutting the tile as if it were an ordinary border tile.

■ Measure the pipe's distance from the edge and mark the back of the tile.

■ On some tiles, you can punch through from the pile side using the pipe offcut and a hammer. Otherwise, draw round the edge of the pipe, then cut out the hole fractionally inside the marked line.

■ Finally, cut a straight line from the hole to the edge of the tile so that you can slip it around the pipe.

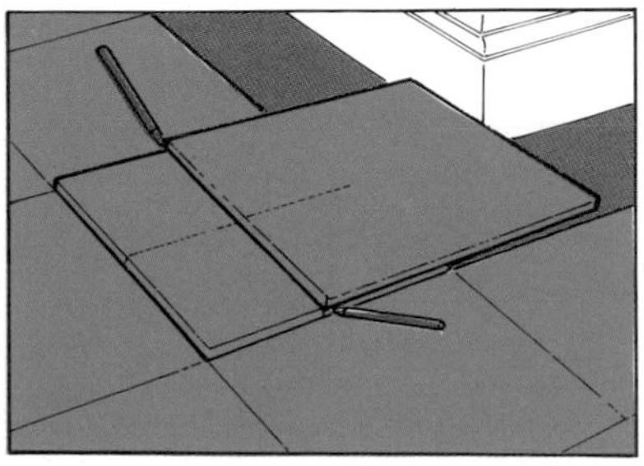

***Use the 'double tile'** technique at corners. Mark one cutting line, then repeat for the other.*

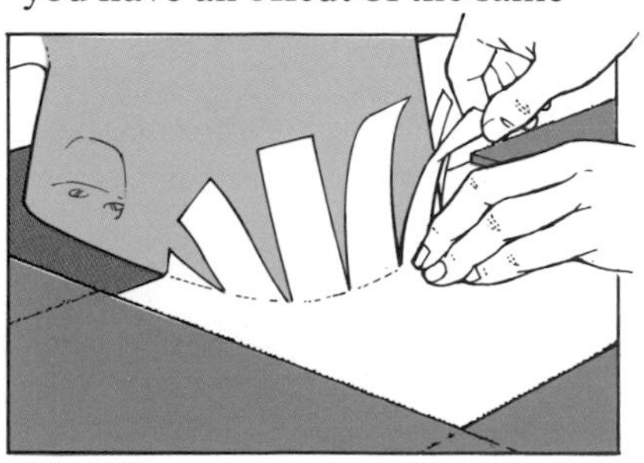

***Use a paper template** for awkward shapes. Clip in around the edges, crease, then trim to fit.*

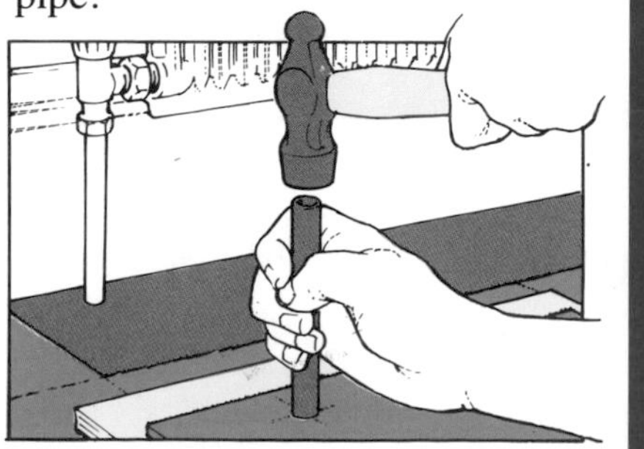

***Try punching through the tile** with an offcut before slitting it to fit around a small pipe.*

LAYING VINYL AND RUBBER TILES

Vinyl floor tiles give a hard wearing, easy-to-clean surface that's ideally suited to splash-prone rooms such as kitchens and bathrooms. And in a room containing lots of awkward corners, they are likely to be considerably easier to lay than a fitted carpet or sheet vinyl; if you do mis-cut, only a single tile gets wasted.

An expensive, but very durable, alternative to conventional vinyl tiles is synthetic rubber stud flooring – originally developed for airports and other public places. This also comes in tile form, and is laid in virtually the same way.

Decorative possibilities

One of the most appealing things about vinyl tiles is that different colours and styles can be mixed to create a range of decorative effects – for example, you could combine a pale, plain-coloured tile for the main floor area with a 'border' of darker patterned tiles.

For the more adventurous, vinyl tiles also lend themselves to being laid diagonally. The techniques for doing so are slightly different from the basic laying method, and are covered separately on page 48.

.... Shopping List ....

Vinyl tiles vary widely in price, from relatively economical to very expensive. Some are solid vinyl, others have a cushioned layer, and patterns vary from gently flecked, soft geometric and floral to imitations of brick, cork and other surfaces.

Practically speaking the main choice is between *self adhesive* and *plain* tiles. Self-adhesive tiles are less messy to lay, but stick instantly and don't allow much margin for error. For plain tiles, always use the adhesive recommended by the makers – and where appropriate, buy a supply of suitable *solvent* for cleaning.

Most vinyl tiles are around 300mm (12″) square, and are sold in packs of varying sizes. Coverage per pack is always given on the packaging, so simply divide this figure into the floor area (measured in square metres) and round up to the nearest whole pack to find the total number of packs required. Don't forget that if the room is an awkward shape, it's easier to divide it into smaller rectangles, work out their areas, then add the figures together.

Rubber stud tiles are generally 500mm (20″) square and come in packs of 4. They must be laid with a heavy-duty neoprene rubber-based adhesive, which means taking extra care over preparing the subfloor (see overleaf).

Tools and other materials: Tape measure, pencil, string, chalk, trimming knife, metal rule or straightedge, notched adhesive spreader (if not supplied with the adhesive), white spirit, a supply of clean rags.

plain vinyl

300   500

self-adhesive vinyl   rubber stud

Vinyl tiles are available in many styles, appropriate for many different situations. In the kitchen (top) they are a practical choice: this fresh, basketweave pattern is a classic style which will not date easily. Softer patterns (above), with floral motifs, are an appropriate choice in a sun room.
Rubber stud flooring gives a stylish look to this bathroom with a sunken bath.

PREPARATION AND PLANNING

The flexibility of vinyl tiles means that any imperfections in the sub-floor soon show through, so take extra care over preparation.

Solid floors should be level, dry and free of dust. For rubber tiles, make doubly certain that the entire surface is stable; the adhesive can all too easily pull up lumps of concrete, causing the tiles to lift.

Suspended wooden floors need lining unless made of chipboard: use hardboard for vinyl; cheap-grade 6mm (¼") plywood for rubber tiles.

Bear in mind that the floor level is bound to be raised to some extent: if doors open into the room take them off their hinges and store ready for trimming after the tiles have been laid; you may also need to fit trim strips across doorways to stop the tiles getting scuffed.

Where to start

As with any sort of floor tiling, you will get better results if you set out the tiles in a dry run, working outwards from a pair of lines drawn at right angles across the middle of the room.

■ Use chalked string to snap the lines, or draw them in pencil, depending on the floor surface.

■ Line number one should be roughly in the middle of the room,

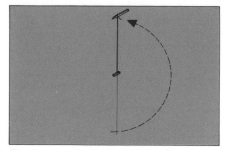

To draw a perfect right angle, take a piece of string with a pencil tied to it and pin one end to the centre of the first setting out line. Draw arcs to cut through both sides of the line . . .

but parallel to the most dominant visual line – for example, a straight wall, bath, or run of kitchen units. (If there is no obvious visual line, take one through the middle of the door.)

■ Line number two should run at right angles to the first one. The steps above show a convenient way to ensure this, by adapting a piece of basic school geometry.

Lay the tiles along the lines and see what gaps are left around the edges of the room. If necessary, re-draw one or both lines in a slightly different position so that the gaps are more or less even in size, with no awkward slivers (ie under a third of a tile's width) to cut.

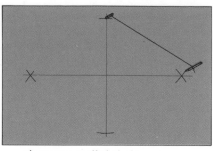

. . . then use a slightly longer piece of string to draw arcs to either side of the setting out line as shown. Join the points at which the arcs cross to form the second setting out line.

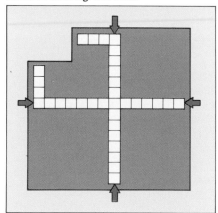

Lay out tiles in a dry run to check the size of the gaps left around the edges of the room. If these fall badly, reposition one or both setting out lines.

Map it out

❛ If you want to combine different coloured tiles to form a pattern, it's much better to work to a scale plan. Initially you can use the plan to try out different designs, and to calculate how many of each sort of tile you need. Later on, use it as a setting out and laying guide.

Draw the plan on 5mm squared paper, available as cheap sketch pads from stationers. For most rooms, a scale of 1:20 will allow you to represent each square as a tile while keeping the plan a manageable size. ❜

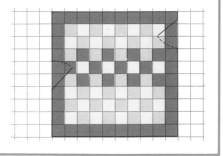

LAYING THE TILES

Check vinyl tiles carefully before you start. Some designs have patterns with a 'right' and a 'wrong' way, so make sure you know which is which; if necessary, lay out all the whole tiles in a dry run and then stack them in the correct laying sequence.

Self-adhesive tiles are less messy to lay, but the backs of the tiles are *very* sticky and can't be slid around if you position them wrongly. When you start, use the tips of your fingers to hold the tiles just above the floor surface, align the edges with the guide lines, then lower gently into place. Smooth down the tiles with a soft cloth, and keep some white spirit handy to wipe any adhesive marks off the face of the tiles.

Lay all the whole tiles before cutting the edge tiles. You can do the cutting straight away, since the adhesive acts instantly. When cutting tiles to fit, make all the necessary cuts before you peel off the backing paper.

Do the cutting on a piece of board, using a sharp trimming knife and a steel rule or metal straightedge. Depending on the thickness of the tile, you may not be able to cut it in one go: make repeated passes instead, and keep the straightedge steady.

Plain tiles can be laid in much the same way, but this time spread an area of adhesive large enough to lay four tiles at a time. At the beginning, take care that the adhesive doesn't obscure the guide lines. Wipe off any excess on the face of the tiles immediately.

Lay all the whole tiles, then leave the adhesive to dry for at least 12 hours before fitting the edge tiles. For cut tiles, glue the tiles themselves, not the floor.

Rubber stud tiles are larger than plain vinyl, and the neoprene adhesive is much stickier. So it's advisable only to spread enough adhesive for one tile at a time.

The tiles are designed to create a 'continuous' floor surface, so lay them staggered to hide the joints.

Start tiling where the setting out lines cross. Position the first tile in the angle, then work outwards over the quadrant furthest from the door.

With self-adhesive tiles, peel off the backing and hold the tile just above the floor. Adjust until its position is correct, then press down and smooth.

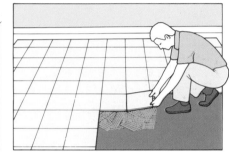

For plain tiles, spread enough adhesive to lay four tiles at a time. Butt the tiles closely, then wipe off any adhesive which squeezes up through the joints.

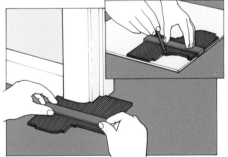

A profile gauge is handy for tricky obstacles: press in place, transfer the shape to the tile, and cut. Then trim the square edge of the tile to fit the gap.

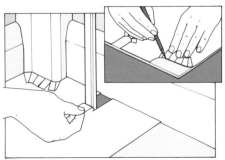

Use sheets of paper the same size as the tiles – or the paper backing on self-adhesive tiles – to make up templates for large obstacles and pipes.

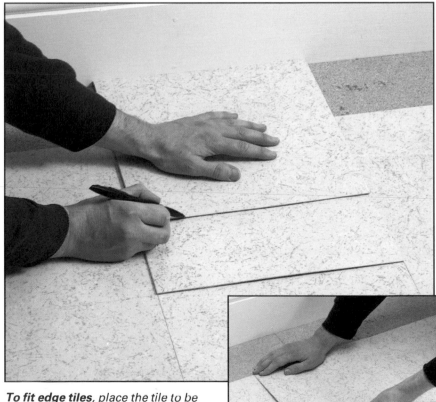

To fit edge tiles, place the tile to be cut on the adjacent, whole tile (inset). Butt a spare tile to the skirting and use the opposite edge to mark the cutting line.

DIAGONAL TILING

Tiling diagonally has the potential for creating a range of interesting pattern effects. In a small, narrow room it can also help to give an impression of greater width.

The actual laying procedure is the same as for tiles laid conventionally – the difference is in the setting out. Start in the usual way, by chalking or drawing lines at right angles across the middle of the room.

■ A total diagonal look (ie with the tiles carried to the edges of the room) works best where the floor is an irregular shape. Problems may still arise if the floor dimensions are such that you're left with lots of fiddly cuts at the edges.

■ The alternative is to 'frame' the diagonal tiling with a border of whole tiles laid square, then fill in the edge gaps in the usual way. This generally works better where the floor is a regular shape.

Setting out

The most reliable way to decide which method looks best is to lay out most of the tiles in a dry run. Start by positioning the first tile on the 'cross' with its points on the setting out lines, then carry the tiles towards the edges.

If you opt for the frame method, mark where the last whole tiles should fall in each quadrant, then lay out the frame tiles. If this leaves awkward gaps around the edges, go back and re-draw the original setting out lines. Use cut tiles in the centre of the border to align the corners exactly.

When the arrangement looks right, chalk or draw further setting out lines around the edges of the room as a position guide for the frame tiles. Check that these are exactly parallel to the original lines.

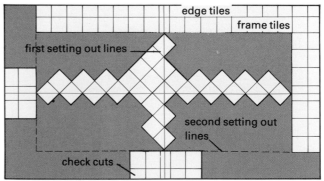

Setting out for a total diagonal look: having positioned the first tile on the 'cross', carry the dry run towards the edges and see what sort of gaps are left. You may be able to avoid fiddly cuts by repositioning the lines.

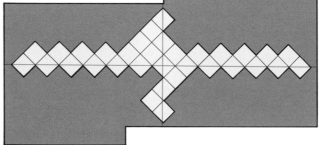

Diagonal tiling adds an extra dimension to a room, drawing the eye to the furthest corners. The effect is less regimented than tiles laid square to the room.

Setting out for a 'framed' look: lay out the frame tiles, then reposition the first setting out lines if necessary to even up the gaps. Follow by drawing further setting out lines, parallel to the originals, around the edges of the room.

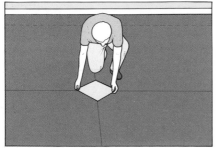

1 *The first tile determines the line of the joints, so make sure you position it accurately with the four points falling on the lines of the 'cross'.*

2 *Continue laying whole tiles diagonally across one quadrant. Then lay whole frame tiles around the edge of the quadrant, following the lines.*

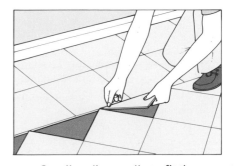

3 *Cut tiles diagonally to fit the gaps inside the frame, then cut and fit the edge tiles in the usual way. Repeat for the other three quadrants.*

LAYING FITTED CARPETS

Laying and fitting carpets yourself isn't always a good idea, particularly on large floors or awkwardly shaped areas such as the stairs. Indeed, many suppliers offer free fitting on carpets over a certain value, and professional laying should ensure you get the best wear out of top quality carpets – which have to be stretched tightly so that the pile stands upright.

Even so, there are times when it simply isn't worth calling in the professionals – for example, when laying a cheap foam backed carpet or remnant. You might also want to take carpets with you if you move.

Laying methods

There are three ways to fix carpets. **Foam backed** carpets are normally held around the edges of the room with *double-sided carpet tape.*

Canvas backed carpets can be stretched on gripper strips tacked to the floor around the edges of the room. Alternatively, if the subfloor is wooden, the edges can simply be turned over and tacked in place.

Underlay and lining

Foam or felt underlay should always be laid under canvas backed carpets to prolong wear and add a luxurious feel. It is unnecessary under foam backed carpets.

An extra lining (of paper or nylon) is essential for canvas backed carpet laid over floorboards, to prevent dirt from being drawn up from the void beneath the floor. And under foam backed carpets, a lining can help to prevent the backing from sticking to the subfloor.

Preparation

The subfloor must be clean and free from grease, particularly if you are using adhesive or carpet tape. Remove any doors for clearance if necessary (see Problem Solver).

Wooden floors should be level, with no movement in the boards and all nails punched home. If the boards are at all uneven, line the floor with hardboard, as for sheet vinyl.

Solid floors must be level and free from damp. If they are slightly uneven, level with self-levelling compound; if they are crumbling or 'out' by more than 12mm (½″), get them rescreeded.

PLANNING AND MEASURING

Before buying, measure the room.

■ Measure the overall area, taking measurements along and across the room at several points to allow for moderate irregularities. Measure into bays and alcoves where appropriate.

■ Check how square the walls are to one another by measuring the diagonals as well; if they are equal, you should have little trouble deciding how much carpet to order. If one diagonal is considerably longer than the other, allow extra width and length to ensure a good fit.

■ Allow at least 100mm (4″) extra all around so you can trim the carpet for an accurate fit.

■ Underlay and lining paper should be laid leaving a 50mm (2″) gap all around for double-sided tape, gripper strips or turning and tacking.

Which way round?

Choose a carpet which is wide enough to fit right across the room if possible. If you do have to join widths, plan the job so that seams fall in the areas of least traffic, and make sure that the pile on each piece runs in the same direction.

■ Check the width of the carpet and decide which way to lay it according to the room's proportions. For example, on a floor measuring 2.5×3.8m (8′2″×12′6″), a single piece of 4m (13′) carpet could run the length of the room.

■ A woven carpet should ideally be laid so that the direction of the pile runs away from the door (and towards the window if possible). This helps to prevent indentations from footmarks showing as you enter the room.

A patterned, tufted carpet in 70/20 wool/nylon is an ideal choice for a living room. Measure across the room at several points (inset) and check the diagonals as well before ordering.

For fixing buy *double-sided tape*, *tacks*, or *carpet gripper strip* according to your chosen method, plus a tack hammer for driving in the nails. Note that grippers come part-nailed, so be sure to state whether you're fixing to floorboards or concrete. *A staple gun* is handy for fixing lining or underlay to wood floors.

For joining seams use *double-sided tape* on foam backed carpet, or *woven tape* and *latex adhesive* on canvas backed carpet. *Single-sided carpet tape* is used to join widths of underlay.

For cutting use *scissors* and/or a *trimming knife*, plus a *metal straight edge* and *tape measure*.

Professional tools aren't essential, but make it easier to get a good finish. Aim to hire or improvise the following items, as they are expensive to buy.

A knee-kicker is used to stretch carpet across the room. The head spikes are adjustable to suit the carpet pile.

Position the kicker head near the edge of the carpet, at a slight angle to the run of the gripper strip. Knock the knee pad to force the carpet closer to the wall, then tuck the edge over the gripper.

A carpet layer's hammer has a long slim head for knocking in nails close to skirtings. It can also be held sideways and used for pressing carpet on to grippers.

A carpet layer's bolster is for tucking carpet between gripper strips and the wall. You can use a clean, blunt bricklayer's bolster or wallpaper scraper instead.

Un-nailed grippers are used in the trade where there's a risk of nailing through pipes. These need a special adhesive – ask your supplier.

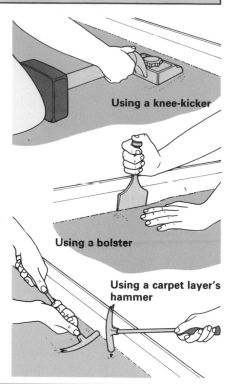

Using a knee-kicker

Using a bolster

Using a carpet layer's hammer

LAYING FOAM-BACKED CARPET

Foam backed carpets are relatively easy to lay – no underlay is used and they don't need stretching.

■ Start by laying the lining if needed. It doesn't have to be fixed, but taping or stapling it in place will stop it shifting around.

■ Check which way the pile runs, and unroll the carpet so it lies the right way round. When it is as flat and smooth as possible, trim to size leaving at least 50mm (2″) lapping up the walls all the way round.

■ Make 'freeing cuts' diagonally into the corners so that the carpet lies as flat as possible.

■ Turn back the edge of the carpet and stick down the tape, leaving the backing paper in place.

■ Start to fit the carpet along one long straight wall. You may be able to butt the edge straight to the wall, but usually it's safer to trim it to fit. Stick the carpet down, unpeeling the tape backing and pulling the carpet tight as you go.

■ With one side held firmly, tread the carpet in place, shuffling across the room to remove wrinkles. Repeat to get the carpet as taut as possible.

■ Trim and fit the opposite edge to the one you fixed, making diagonal cuts to fit it into internal or external corners. Stick it in place.

■ Finally, work up and down the room in the same way and stick the remaining edges.

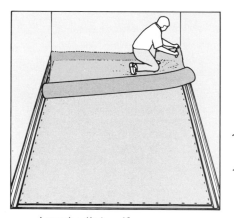

1 Lay the lining if necessary, stapling or sticking it with double-sided tape. Align the end of the carpet with the wall and unroll. Trim waste to 50mm (2″).

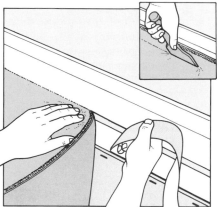

2 Position tape on the floor around the edge of the lining paper. Use a bolster to mark the trim line: ensure the carpet is taut before cutting and sticking.

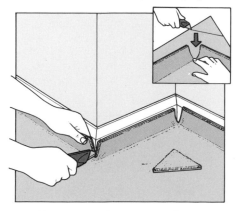

3 Cut across the carpet where it is to fit into internal corners before trimming. At external corners, cut diagonally to the obstruction.

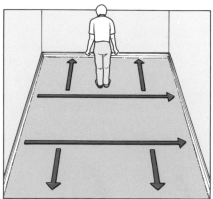

4 Tread the carpet in place across the room, then stick the opposite edge. Finally, work up and down the room and stick the remaining edges in place.

LAYING CANVAS BACKED CARPETS

Canvas backed carpets should be stretched tightly across the room, whether they are turned and tacked or fitted to gripper strips. You can stretch the carpet by shuffling it into place with your feet, but for a professional finish hire a knee-kicker. Proper tensioning ensures that the pile stands as upright as possible, improving its life. Some types of carpet also tend to stretch as they wear in; tensioning should prevent this too.

Lay the lining and underlay first, with a 50mm (2") border. If using grippers, fix them and any threshold strips (see overleaf) next. Watch out for buried pipes and cables.

Before stretching and fitting the carpet, trim it to fit the room allowing about 100mm (4") extra all around. Then, starting from one corner, trim the waste to 20mm (¾") along adjacent edges. Fix these edges for 300mm (1') out from the corner, then stretch the carpet and fit it to the gripper strips along the longer wall. Next stretch it along the shorter wall, out from the same corner. Stretch the carpet across the room towards the corner opposite the starting point, then fit along the remaining walls.

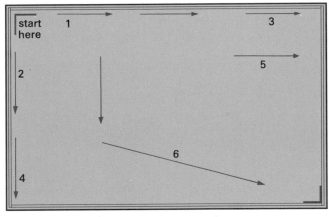

The basic stretching plan is to start from one corner. Fix firmly on both sides of the corner, then stretch and fit along each adjacent wall. Stretch down the longer wall to the opposite corner before fitting the carpet along the remaining walls.

1 *Lay the lining and then the underlay, fixing them with staples or tape. Join seams with carpet tape. Nail gripper strips around the room about 5mm (¼") from the wall. At curves, cut short lengths of strip leaving at least two nails for fixing.*

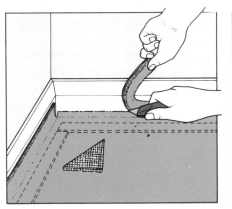

2 *Unroll the carpet and trim to fit roughly. At the starting corner, trim diagonally across it. Trim the waste to 19mm (¾") and press over the gripper strip.*

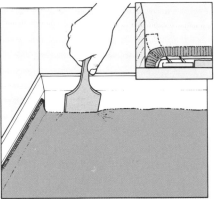

3 *Tuck the edge waste between the gripper and skirting. Stretch the carpet along the first edge, pressing it on to the gripper and tucking in as you go.*

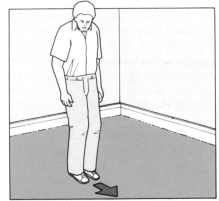

4 *Work around the room in the order shown above, treading the carpet as flat as possible before stretching it taut and fitting over the grippers.*

Working with tufteds

❝If tufted carpets are stored in an unheated place, the backing stiffens up. Leave the carpet in a warm room so that it becomes pliable again – particularly if you plan to lay the carpet in an awkward area. Never fold a tufted carpet, as you will have great difficulty removing the creases. ❞

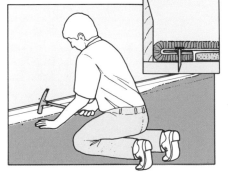

If turning and tacking fit the first corner by turning under about 50mm (2") and tacking it in place every 100mm (4"). Trim away excess fabric across the corner.

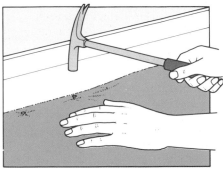

Continue to turn and tack along one edge, stretching it as you go. Repeat for the other edge. Then stretch the carpet across the room, trim, turn and tack.

JOINING WIDTHS

Traditionally, seams between widths of carpet were sewn. Nowadays adhesives and carpet tape are more commonly used. Where possible, join machined edges; otherwise, overlap the two edges to be joined and use one edge as a cutting guide to trim the layer underneath.

With foam backed carpets use the same double-sided tape used to fix the carpet but strengthen the joint with latex adhesive.

With woven backings use woven tape and latex adhesive to make the join. You should join widths before stretching the carpet to fit.

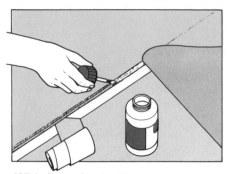

With foam backed carpets position the tape on the floor along the seam line. Apply latex adhesive along the cut edge, peel off the backing and press firmly.

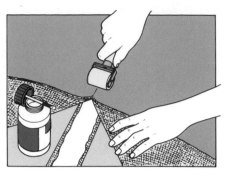

For canvas backed carpet lay woven tape along the seam line, coat it with adhesive, then press the edges in place. Roll the seam afterwards for a good bond.

THRESHOLD STRIPS

Choose a threshold strip *without* spikes for foam backed carpet, *with* spikes for gripper fixing. The type of strip is also governed by what's on the other side of the doorway: where carpets butt up to each other, use a double-sided strip designed to hold carpets on both sides; use a single-sided strip if the carpet finishes here

The threshold strip should be fitted directly under the position of the door when closed. But if there is a hard floorcovering on the other side of the door, the threshold strip must cover its edge.

Position the carpet over the strip, mark the cutting line and trim any waste. Then simply tuck the edge under the cover strip.

To hold foam backed carpets in place, hammer the strip over the dge of the carpet using a piece of wood to protect the metal surface.

▉PROBLEM SOLVER▉

Problems with doors

Laying a thick new carpet could involve removing and trimming any inward-opening doors.

■ To remove a door, open it wide and slip magazines underneath to take the weight while you release the hinges.

■ After fitting the carpet, measure down the frame from the lower hinge to the surface of the new carpet, and compare this with the equivalent measurement on the door. Mark the bottom edge for trimming.

■ To trim a small amount – less than 6mm (¼″) or so – simply plane down to the marked line.

■ To trim more, use a panel saw and plane smooth, or use a power plane.

■ Check the fit of the door by holding both open and closed. If all is well, place it back on the magazines to align the hinge plates, then refit the screws.

Support the door with magazines while unscrewing the hinges.

Measure and mark the amount to be trimmed.

Plane to the marked line.

LIFTING AND REPAIRING FLOORBOARDS

Floorboards which creak or wobble are both a nuisance and a potential danger. And splinters, bumps or protruding nail heads will shorten the life of any floorcovering laid over the top.

Faults like these can often be put right quite easily using only basic tools, once the offending boards have been exposed. But sometimes during the course of repairs it's necessary to lift and replace boards – a job calling for much more specialized tools and techniques. The same applies if you need to get to the cavity under the floor – for example, to lay pipes or cables.

Loose boards creak at best, and at worst may trip someone up. Punch all existing nails below the surface, then drive in extra nails (preferably proper *flooring brads*) or secure with countersunk screws.

If the creaking persists, try driving a short, thick countersunk screw **between** the boards to jam them together.

Knots are harder and less prone to shrinkage than the wood around them, which often leads to bumps. Level them with a plane or Surform – if you try to sand them, you're likely to remove more of the surrounding wood.

Watch out for concealed cables or pipes which may be notched into the tops of the joists. They should have been laid in the centre of the boards, so always nail about 20mm (¾") from each side.

POSSIBLE FAULTS AND SIMPLE REPAIRS

Nail heads may protrude due to wear or shrinkage of the boards. Hammer level and punch just below the surface. If the boards are to be left exposed, fill the indents with a slightly darker wood filler – it's less noticeable than a light one.

Broken or split boards are dangerous – remove and replace.

Sagging points to problems in the supporting joists. See Problem Solver overleaf.

Warped boards can be trimmed to remove high spots using a Surform or power sander. If the warping is bad, it's easier to replace.

Splintering may have developed in an old board. If minor, glue the loose pieces with woodworking adhesive and clamp in position with a weight on a plastic bag to stop it sticking. Otherwise, replace the board.

Gaps cause draughts. They also look unsightly if left exposed, and can set up ridges in carpet laid over them. Fill with wood or papier mâché (see below) or cover with hardboard before laying carpet.

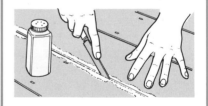

Trade tip

Stopping squeaks

6 *Squeaking in floorboards is often the result of two boards rubbing together. Where this is the case, lubricate the gap between the boards by puffing in talcum powder or French chalk and working it down with an old table knife blade – the squeak should soon stop.* 9

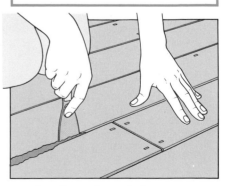

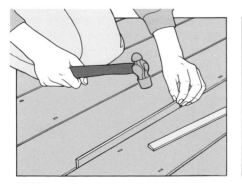

Fill large gaps between boards with strips of wood shaped to a slight taper. Coat with glue and hammer into the gap, then plane level after the glue dries.

Fill narrow gaps with papier-mâché. Mix up some torn-up newspaper, wallpaper paste and boiling water (you can also add wood stain to match the boards) . . .

. . . then force the pulp between the boards with a filling knife. Leave the filler slightly proud of the surface, then sand it smooth when hard.

LIFTING INDIVIDUAL BOARDS

Lifting floorboards which have been lifted before isn't generally too difficult: neither end will be trapped, so once you've checked for extra screw fixings you can simply insert a bolster or crowbar into the gaps and lever gently.

Removing a full-length board is a different matter. One or both ends will be trapped under skirtings or partition walls, so before you can lift it you have to saw through it somewhere along its length.

First, check whether the board is square edged or tongued and grooved (T&G): poke a blade between the gaps and see if it slips through easily; if it stops halfway, the board is T&G and you need to saw through the tongues on both sides to release it.

There are two ways of sawing through the board itself:
■ Over a joist, using a special curved-bladed floorboard saw or a tenon saw.
■ Next to a joist, using a jigsaw. This is much quicker, but risks harming underfloor cables or pipes. Adjusting the sole plate on the saw to cut at an angle of 30° gives a much neater join. For extra safety, cut over a block of wood as shown below to restrict the blade depth.

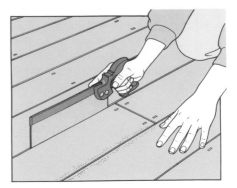

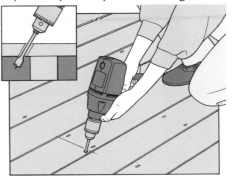

For T&G boards, saw a short way down both sides to sever the tongues using a tenon saw or floorboard saw. The rest should split away when you start lifting.

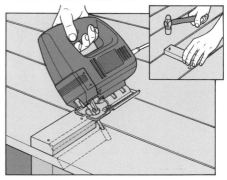

To saw beside a joist, find the edge of the joist with a blade and mark a cutting line across the board. Drill a hole big enough to admit the sawblade . . .

To saw over a joist, look for the rows of nails indicating its position and mark a cutting line just inside one of the rows. Cut along the line using short, flat strokes, then if necessary sever the unreachable ends using a woodworking chisel.

. . . then nail a block of wood parallel with the line. Adjust the jigsaw sole plate to 30°, insert the blade, and saw through the block and board together.

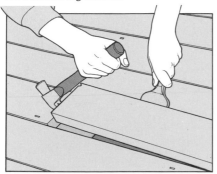

1 To lift the severed board, prise up the cut end from one side using a bolster. Apply enough force to get the jaws of a claw hammer under the end.

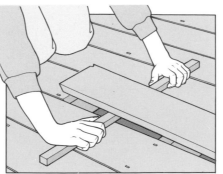

2 Continue levering until you can slide a length of batten under the raised board. Using both hands, force the batten towards the next joist.

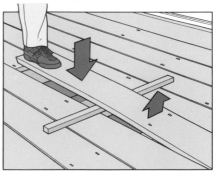

3 When the batten will go no further, put your weight on the cut end to 'spring' the board from the next joist. Repeat this until you reach the end.

PATCHING IN A NEW BOARD

Floorboards exist in a range of widths and thicknesses, but if you're only patching the odd section there is little point searching timber merchants for an exact match. Instead, buy the nearest size you can find and then adapt it to fit:
■ If the board is too wide, plane down the edges to a slight taper.
■ If the board is too thick, mark the joist positions and then cut shallow notches with a chisel.
■ If the board is too thin, fit cardboard or plywood packing over the joists before fixing.

Where you've sawn beside a joist, screw on a batten to support the replacement board before fixing. Screw, rather than nail, the board for future access.

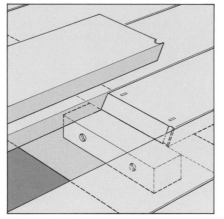
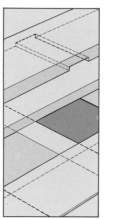
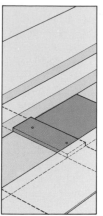

If you've sawn next to a joist, screw a batten to the side of the joist to support the new board. Bevel the end of the board if you cut the old section at an angle.

Notch a board which is too thick where it passes over the joists. *Pack underneath* a board which is too thin using slips of cardboard or plywood.

■ PROBLEM SOLVER

Problems with joists

Numerous warped, split or damaged boards – or serious sagging in the floor as a whole – point to faults in the floor joists below. Joist problems are more common on ground floors, where the danger of damp is ever-present. But in any event, it's worth checking on the condition of the joists whenever you have to lift more than one or two boards.

Rot or woodworm should be immediately obvious, and need prompt treatment. Any signs of dampness, dark staining or general deterioration suggest that the joists are beginning to rot, in which case they can be rescued if caught in time. By far the best course of action is to have a damp/rot survey carried out by a preservation specialist.

Sagging in an otherwise sound joist could be due to one of several things:
■ Overloading, either now or at some time in the past.
■ Over-weakening, where the joist has been notched to take pipe and cable runs.
■ Weakness in the timber itself.

These faults can usually be cured by strengthening the joist with a new section of timber, or by bracing it against its neighbours with timber struts. Bear in mind, however, that you may have to remove a considerable number of boards to gain sufficient access for putting in the struts.

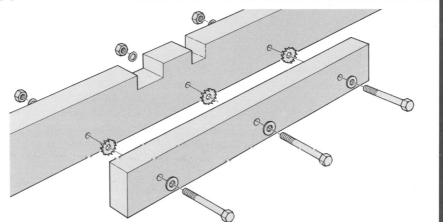

Strengthen a weakened joist by coach-bolting a matching piece of timber alongside it. The new section should be at least 900mm (3') long to be effective. Bolt at 300mm (12") intervals, using star washers (timber connectors) between the sections to lock them together.

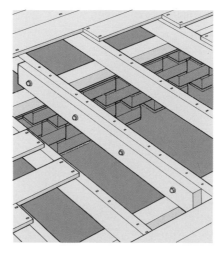
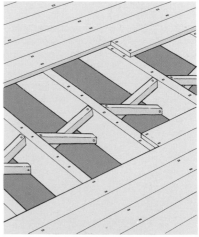

On a ground floor only, you may be able to strengthen a sagging joist by coach-bolting a new section of timber to it and supporting the ends on the two nearest sleeper walls . . .

. . . alternatively, for all joists make up herringbone struts from lengths of 50×50mm (2×2") timber. Nail the struts between the affected joist and its neighbours at 600mm (2') intervals.

RELAYING FLOORBOARDS

Relaying larger areas of floorboards is generally more difficult and disruptive than replacing individual sections. Although it's easy to prise up the boards once the first one is out of the way, you have to make sure the ends are free before you can lift them.

Where the boards are trapped by a skirting, remove this first: prise it away from its wall fixings with a bolster or crowbar, using a block of wood for leverage. Where boards disappear under a partition wall, you have no choice but to saw them off at the nearest convenient joist.

Replacing boards

With the boards up, pull out the old nails and then repair any boards that are salvageable. Boards with only surface damage can often be re-used the other way up.

Take a sample of board with you when buying replacements. New boards are stocked by timber and builders' merchants, but for older properties you may be better off going to an architectural salvage yard for secondhand boards.

Relaying

The main problem when relaying a number of floorboards – especially the square-edged type – is forcing them tightly together so that the gaps are as small as possible. There are two ways of doing this: with a pair of folding wedges (which you can make), or using a *floorboard cramp* (which you can hire).

In both cases it's worth buying a supply of purpose-made *flooring brads*, which are generally sold by the pound or ½kg (equivalent to around 80 2″ nails). Use brads at least twice as long as the boards are thick, allowing two per joist. Screw down any boards which you might need to lift for access in the future (and if they are T&G, saw off the tongues).

Joints and edges

Aim to relay the boards with as few joints as possible, and vary the lengths so that no two joints are next to each other. Wedge or cramp after every four or five boards.

If you're relaying the whole floor, decide whether or not you need to remove the side skirtings; often, they can be left in place and the edge boards slipped underneath.

When you reach the far side of the room, you may have to cut the last board along its length to fit the gap. There's no need to do this neatly, as the cut edge will be concealed by the skirting.

With T&G boards, start with the groove side towards the wall. At the far side, lock the last three boards together and 'spring' them under the skirting before fixing.

Trade tip

Shrinking new boards

6 When buying new floorboards, check that they are thoroughly seasoned or they may warp after fixing. In all cases, leave replacement boards stacked in the room they are going in for at least two days before laying. This will help them acclimatize, and minimize the risk of shrinkage in the future. 9

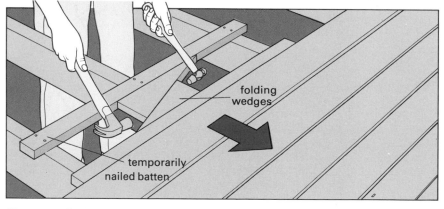

If you use folding wedges to pack the boards, nail a batten temporarily across the joists and place an offcut against the edge of the nearest board. Drive in the wedges from both sides to force the boards tightly together. Repeat every four or five boards.

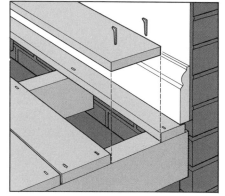

A square-edged end board may have to be sawn along its length and slid underneath the skirting to hide the cut edge. Do this before nailing the previous board.

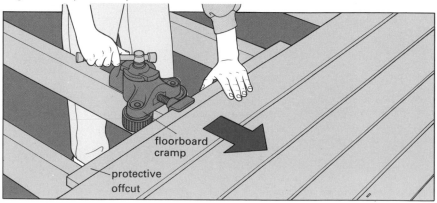

If you use a floorboard cramp, start by positioning the tool on a convenient joist and tightening the clamp. Place an offcut against the floorboards being packed, then turn the handle on the clamp to force them tightly together. Take care not to over-clamp.

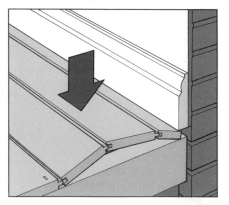

T&G boards should be interlocked and 'sprung' under the skirting as shown. Again, you may have to cut down the last board to fit the remaining gap.

STRIPPING AND SEALING FLOORBOARDS

In older homes, the original pine floorboards (or, if you are very lucky, oak ones) can be sanded and sealed to give a warm, natural finish that provides the perfect complement to rugs or loose-laid carpet. Sanding and sealing is also among the most economical ways of finishing a floor, although equipment hire and the cost of the sealant can push up the price further than you might expect. Much depends, too, on the condition of the boards: if they are badly damaged or deeply stained already, lining them with hardboard and laying a budget floorcovering such as sheet vinyl or foam-backed carpet is likely to be more sensible.

If you decide to go ahead, make sure you are well prepared. Clear the room completely of furnishings and ensure that any repairs to the boards have been carried out before committing yourself to hire charges.

■ Punch nails below the surface and fill large gaps.
■ Replace or turn over damaged and stained boards.

The same principles apply to sanding and refinishing other types of wood floor, such as solid wood strip and traditional parquet.

Old floorboards in almost any condition can be renovated and sealed to give a durable floor surface.

.... Shopping List....

Floor sanding equipment can be hired from virtually any hire shop. You need a *floor sanding machine* to deal with the main area, plus an *edging sander* for finishing the edges and any awkward corners. (If you have an orbital sander this may do instead, but it will take heavy punishment).

The hire shop should supply *abrasive sheets* to fit both machines on a sale-or-return basis. Ask for a mixture of coarse, medium and fine grades in both cases.

Protective gear is essential for floor sanding, which is a very noisy and messy job. Make sure you have a dust mask, ear defenders, overalls, and goggles.

Sealant may also be sold by the hire shop, though a DIY store will offer a wider selection.

Polyurethane varnish is the usual choice. It is economical, but slow to dry and picks up dust easily; you need at least 3 (and preferably 4) coats. *Two-part plastic coating* is tougher and dries within the hour, but is more unpleasant to apply and can work out costlier, even though you only need 2 coats. An *oleo-resinous sealant* is the best choice if you plan to give the floor a wax polished finish, though this will be hard work to maintain. You could also consider staining or coloured varnish (see overleaf).

When buying sealant, be sure to check the recommended coverage per coat. For polyurethane, you need white spirit for thinning.

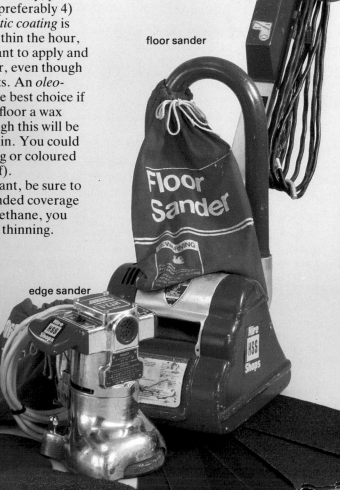

floor sander

oleo-resinous sealant

edge sander

sealant

two-part plastic coating

polyurethane varnish

protective gear

SANDING THE FLOOR

The dust and noise raised by sanding a floor can be considerable, so warn family and neighbours. Immediately before you start:

■ Double-check that the boards are firmly fixed and that there are no sharp nail heads or screws protruding above the surface.

■ Seal up the cracks around doors with parcel tape, and block the gaps underneath with newspaper.

■ Keep any windows open while actually sanding. Close them again after each stage, and vacuum to keep the dust level down.

Follow the sanding sequence shown on the right, checking the abrasive sheets every so often to make sure they're not clogged. With badly marked floors, work diagonally in both directions before working along the grain. Don't change to fine abrasives until all the marks have gone.

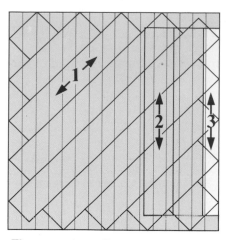

The correct sanding sequence.
Start with the floor sander and work diagonally across the boards using coarse, then medium, abrasives (1). Next, run along the grain of the boards using medium, then fine, abrasives (2). Switch to the edge sander (3): use coarse and medium abrasive to clear the marks; fine to finish.

Trade tip

Using a drum sander

❛ Floor sanders are powerful machines, to be used with care.
■ Always unplug before changing abrasive sheets.
■ Make sure the sheet is taut and firmly locked in place.
■ Never start the machine while the drum is in contact with the ground. Rock the machine back to lift it, then lower gradually when it reaches full speed. Be prepared for it to pull forward.
■ Similarly, rock back to lift the drum before switching off.
■ Empty the dust bag regularly; they have been known to catch fire spontaneously if allowed to become over-full.
■ If the sheet catches on a nail it may shatter with a resounding bang, so be prepared. ❜

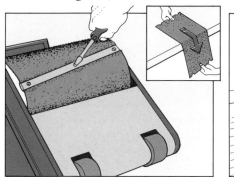

The floor sander sheets *are wrapped over the drum, and held by a screw-down bar. Scrape the backing over the edge of a bench to give the sheet a curl before fitting, then pull it taut.*

The sander *will naturally pull away from you. Use it like a lawn mower and keep the lead over your shoulder so it is out of the way. Avoid 'resting' during a pass, as you risk gouging the boards.*

Use the edge sander *running in the direction of the grain wherever possible, and keep it flat to avoid score marks. Take care not to scrape the disc against the skirtings.*

FINISHING AND SEALING

However you plan to seal the surface, leave the bare boards for as long as possible – and at least a day – to give the dust a chance to settle. (A few squirts into the air with an indoor plant spray will help to speed up the process). Afterwards vacuum the floor thoroughly, along with the skirtings, door and window frames, and any other places where dust might have collected.

Immediately before sealing, wipe over the floor with a cloth soaked in white spirit (don't use water, as this raises the wood grain).

Polyurethane varnish should be thinned with white spirit on the first coat, following the maker's instructions. This allows it to soak into the grain of the wood.

Close all doors and windows. Apply the varnish running with the grain, using a 100mm (4″) brush.

After each coat, sand the surface lightly using fine glasspaper on a block, or a wad of medium grade steel wool. Vacuum again and wipe over with the white-spirit-soaked cloth before applying the next coat.

Two-part coatings give off strong fumes, so keep the room well ventilated; put sheets over windows to stop dust entering.

Mix the coating in the container in which it is supplied following the maker's instructions. Apply with a brush that you won't want to use again – it will be ruined – or use a sponge mop. Sand, if necessary, and vacuum between coats.

Oleo-resinous sealants do not need mixing or thinning. Decant the sealant into a paint kettle and apply with a large brush.

Trade tip

Adding colour

❛ The natural tones of the wood can be altered by staining, or by using coloured polyurethane varnish.
■ Apply the stain before sealing: use a spirit-based stain, and apply it with a cloth pad, not a brush. This gives a more even coverage.
■ If using coloured varnish, choose the gloss type. Apply a thinned coat of clear varnish first. This seals the surface so that it will absorb the colour evenly, then follow with two or more coloured coats. Finish with another clear coat – gloss, matt or silk, according to your preference. ❜

LAYING WOOD MOSAIC FLOORING

The most economical form of hardwood flooring comes as square mosaic panels in a basketweave pattern. These panels are often referred to as 'parquet' or 'woodblock', but they are much thinner and easier to lay than the brick-sized tongued and grooved blocks used on a traditional parquet floor.

The fingers of hardwood making up the panels are generally stuck together with a felt, net or paper backing, though some are strung together with wires which makes cutting slightly trickier. Both methods allow room for expansion and contraction of the wood itself – always the major consideration with a solid wood floor.

Even so, you should ensure the sub-floor is perfectly dry, as well as firm and level. Lift any existing floorcovering and remove all traces of the old adhesive. A concrete floor will probably then need refinishing with self-levelling compound; level a wooden floor with hardboard.

As with other types of wood flooring, you have to leave a small expansion gap around the edges of the room. One way to hide this is to remove the skirtings and notch the door architraves before you start, or you can cover the gap with cork strip or moulding (see below).

Warm and welcoming, hardwood mosaic panels (above) provide a long-lasting and naturally resilient floorcovering for relatively little cost.

....Shopping List....

Wood mosaic panels These are usually sold in packs to cover about 2 square metres, although this varies from supplier to supplier. Allow a few extra panels in case you cut them badly. Always check the panels are square, by comparing them carefully, turning through 90° to check they are square in both directions.

There are two finishes, sealed and unsealed. When making a choice, bear in mind that the *sealed* panels probably have a better surface than you could apply, and you will save a lot of time because you will not have to apply coats and wait for them to dry before using the room.

With *unsealed* panels, you have to finish them yourself: the varnish will bring out darker and richer tones in the wood.

Adhesive Check the maker's recommendations given with the flooring. You may be able to use a PVA-based general *flooring adhesive*, but many types require a heavier black *bituminous adhesive* to protect the wood from moisture.

Sealant Unsealed panels must have a protective finish, while sealed ones will benefit from an extra coat after laying to stop moisture penetrating the joints.

Polyurethane varnish is the usual choice. Alternatives include quick-drying *two-part lacquer*, which is very hardwearing but considerably more expensive, and *oleo-resinous sealant* which provides a good base for wax polish.

Trim materials The expansion gap around the edge of the room can be filled with *compressible cork strip* (usually stocked by the flooring supplier) or covered with softwood *quadrant* or *scotia moulding*. Avoid using cork strip in small rooms, however, as it detracts from the floor's appearance.

Use moulding or *aluminium threshold strip* to finish the floor at doorways.

Tools checklist: Pencil, tape measure, string and chalk, trimming knife, tenon saw, work bench and hacksaw or pliers (for wired panels), sanding equipment, paintbrush. Extra woodworking tools may be needed for finishing the edges and fitting trim strips.

LAYING THE PANELS

Before you start, double-check that the floor surface is completely smooth. Sand down bumps, punch nail heads below the surface, and vacuum thoroughly.

As with conventional floor tiles, lay the panels in dry runs outwards from the centre of the room so that you can start at a point which avoids fiddly cuts. (Professionals often start in a corner which is easier for them but trickier for DIY). Note these points when setting out:

■ In a room where the walls are square to each other, the joints between panels should run parallel to them.

■ If the walls are not square, align the joints with the most dominant feature – the longest wall, or a row of units, for example.

■ Allow for a 10mm (⅜″) expansion gap (or thereabouts) around the edges of the room.

■ Where cuts are unavoidable, try to confine them to the least obvious parts of the room. Aim to make cuts along the joints between the individual fingers, rather than across the fingers themselves (which is more difficult).

■ If you need underfloor access – to a stopcock, for example – ensure the mosaic panel joints coincide with those of the panel in the floor, even if this means more cutting.

Trade tip

Avoiding problems

❝ Half the problems with wood mosaic floors are caused by laying the panels straight from a cold warehouse: in a centrally heated home, they are likely to expand or contract quite dramatically to start with.

Anticipate this by buying the panels at least two days before you plan to lay them. Unwrap them and stack them in the room they are going in so that the wood has a chance to acclimatize. ❞

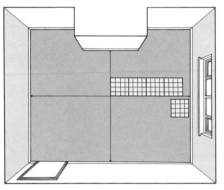

1 Fix string lines at right angles across the centre of the floor and lay dry runs of panels to check the fit at the edges. Aim for cuts to coincide with the joints between 'fingers'.

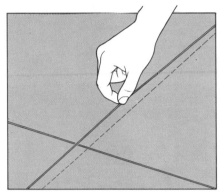

2 When the fit is as good as you can possibly get it, cover the string lines with chalk and snap them to leave guidelines across the floor. Start laying in the quadrant furthest from the door.

3 Starting where the lines cross, spread adhesive over an area slightly larger than a single panel. Position the first panel against the lines.

4 Spread another panel-sized patch of adhesive, then position the second panel so that it butts tightly against the first. Continue spreading and laying, a panel at a time. Avoid letting adhesive squeeze out of the joints on to the surface of the wood.

5 Complete the first quadrant, laying all the whole panels, then work on the other quadrants, finishing at the door. Leave to dry before walking on the panels.

60

CUTTING PANELS

Cut along the joints between fingers wherever possible. On backed panels, you can simply slice through the backing to separate them. Panels which are wired together along grooves on the underside of the fingers can be severed with tin snips, pincers or a junior hacksaw.

Cutting across the fingers themselves is a little more tricky due to the flexibility of the panels.

■ Begin by marking the cutting line, preferably in pencil.
■ Place the panel on a workbench over an offcut of hardboard. The cutting line should just overhang the edge of the bench.
■ Place a batten on top, as near to the cutting line as you can, and clamp in place.

The panel will now be rigid enough to cut accurately (saw through the hardboard at the same time). Use an electric jigsaw, tenon saw or coping saw as appropriate.

In awkward areas, it may be easier to separate the panels into single fingers and then trim these individually to fit (but avoid it if you can, since it's difficult to align them). Trim back the backing material to avoid fouling the joints.

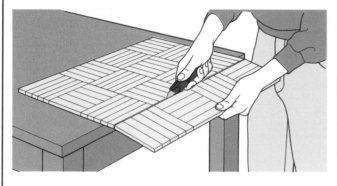

Cut through the backing with a trimming knife to separate individual fingers.

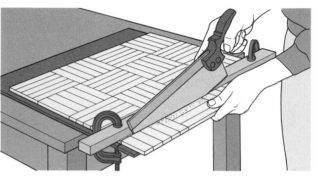

Clamp panels between an offcut of hardboard and a batten to cut across fingers.

FINISHING AROUND THE EDGES

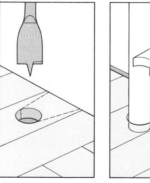

1 To check how much to trim around edge panels, lay the panel to be cut on the last complete panel, then use a spare panel to mark the cutting line.

2 At a pipe, mark its position on the panel and drill a hole of a slightly larger diameter. Follow by cutting out a wedge to fit behind the pipe.

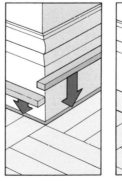

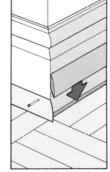

3 Around architrave, either cut a paper template, or use a profile gauge to copy the shape. Transfer to the panel, then cut (preferably with a jigsaw).

4 Finish edges by pressing cork strip into the expansion gap. Alternatively, cover the gap with softwood moulding tacked to the bottom of the skirting board.

5 At doorways, you can fit a tapered moulding or hardwood fillet to stop feet catching on the edge of the floor. Or, use an aluminium threshold strip.

SEALING THE FLOOR

After laying and finishing the edges, the final stage is to seal the panels with varnish or lacquer.

Using polyurethane, unsealed panels need at least three coats. Thin the first coat with white spirit to help it soak in.

Sand and vacuum thoroughly between coats. You can use fine glasspaper on a sanding block, or even a power sander, but many professionals prefer to use a large wad of medium grade steel wool.

Sealed panels require just a single coat, applied unthinned.

1 *Thin the first coat with 1 part white spirit to 10 parts polyurethane. Sand between coats using a wad of medium grade steel wool, then vacuum well.*

2 *As the finish builds up, the rich tones of the wood will start to emerge. Before the final coat, take extra precautions against dust: close any windows, then vacuum the floor and wipe over the surface with a damp cloth.*

■ PROBLEM SOLVER ■

Repairing damaged panels

It's worth keeping a few spare mosaic panels in case of accidental damage – dents from sharp, heavy objects are the most likely cause. In severe cases, you may have to replace an entire panel; it's more likely that the damage is confined to one or two fingers.

■ On backed panels, the fingers can be loosened by scoring around the edges with a trimming knife. With wired panels, you have to sever the wires by tapping sharply along the joints with a bolster or an old wood chisel.

■ Afterwards, prise out the fingers with a claw hammer or old chisel, using an offcut to protect the surrounding surface. Scrape away all traces of the backing and adhesive below.

■ Cut new fingers from a spare panel and check the fit.

With unsealed panels bed the new fingers in place on a fresh layer of adhesive. (If you haven't the correct type, woodworking adhesive should do).

Leave the repair for a couple of days to let the patch acclimatize. If it stands proud, sand level with the surrounding surface, taking care not to remove wood from the other fingers. Finally, sand the entire panel and revarnish.

With sealed panels, check if the replacement fingers stand proud of the surrounding surface. If they do, peel off any backing and sand them on the back to allow them to lie flush when bedded in adhesive. When stuck, sand the top lightly and give one coat of varnish to blend with the surrounding panel.

Sever wired fingers by tapping sharply along the joints with a thin bladed bolster, old wood chisel, or stripping knife. Use a trimming knife on backed panels.

Lever out the damaged fingers with a claw hammer or an old chisel. Afterwards, scrape away all traces of the old adhesive and backing.

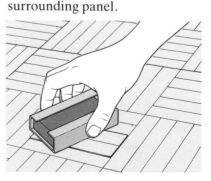

Sand the patched area if necessary, then sand the entire panel so that any colour change in the finish occurs between the panel joints.

LAYING WOODSTRIP FLOORING

Woodstrip is among the most naturally attractive and resilient forms of floorcovering. It is by no means cheap, but most manufacturers claim a life of at least 10 years for the original finish, after which in most cases the surface can be stripped and resealed.

The actual form of the woodstrip (and often the fixing method) varies from one brand to another. Mostly this depends on how the maker deals with the problem of wood's tendency to expand or contract according to the moisture in the atmosphere.

Laminated woodstrip consists of a thin top layer of lacquered or PVC-coated hardwood over a thicker layer of softwood or HDF (high density fibreboard); some types have a third backing layer as well – either HDF or synthetic. The layers are glued together at right angles – like plywood – so that movement in one layer is resisted by the others.

Woodstrip like this may be made up into narrow boards, two or three strips wide, or into panels of narrower strips – often arranged in patterns to resemble parquet. Thicknesses range from 6mm (¼″) to 22m (⅞″); widths and lengths vary according to the manufacturer, the pattern, and the type of wood used for the surface veneer.

Solid woodstrip consists of narrow strips of hardwood which are factory-jointed into wider 'boards' of two or three strips each. The wood is kiln-dried and sealed with polyurethane lacquer to prevent movement, but remains susceptible to external sources of dampness.

Details differ, but in one popular system the edges are tongued and grooved, and there is a groove in the underside to take clips which hold the boards together. Board width in this system averages 130mm (5¼″); lengths are random.

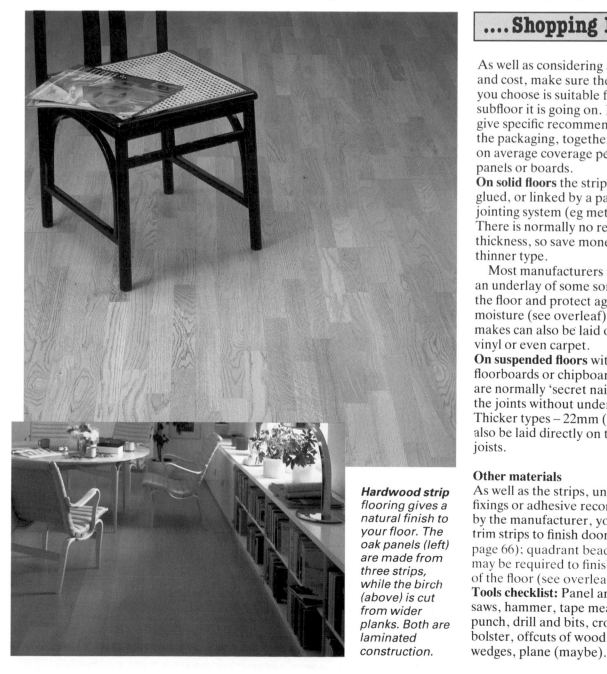

Hardwood strip flooring gives a natural finish to your floor. The oak panels (left) are made from three strips, while the birch (above) is cut from wider planks. Both are laminated construction.

....Shopping List....

As well as considering appearance and cost, make sure the woodstrip you choose is suitable for the subfloor it is going on. Most makers give specific recommendations on the packaging, together with guides on average coverage per pack of panels or boards.

On solid floors the strips are either glued, or linked by a patented jointing system (eg metal clips). There is normally no restriction on thickness, so save money by using a thinner type.

Most manufacturers recommend an underlay of some sort to cushion the floor and protect against moisture (see overleaf); some makes can also be laid over sheet vinyl or even carpet.

On suspended floors with floorboards or chipboard, the strips are normally 'secret nailed' through the joints without underlay. Thicker types – 22mm (⅞″) – can also be laid directly on top of the joists.

Other materials
As well as the strips, underlay, and fixings or adhesive recommended by the manufacturer, you will need trim strips to finish doorways (see page 66); quadrant beading or cork may be required to finish the edges of the floor (see overleaf).

Tools checklist: Panel and tenon saws, hammer, tape measure, nail punch, drill and bits, crowbar or bolster, offcuts of wood for making wedges, plane (maybe).

PREPARING THE FLOOR

Movement in a woodstrip floor can never be eliminated entirely, so when laying the strips you need to leave a small gap – usually about 10mm (3/8") – around the edge of the room to allow for expansion.

The neatest way of doing this is to remove the skirtings before laying the floor so that the expansion gap will be covered. If you cannot (or don't want to) remove the skirtings, the alternatives are to fill the gap with compressible cork strip (available where you buy the woodstrip), or cover it with quadrant beading.

Concrete subfloors must be dry and level. Most manufacturers recommend two underlays: a layer of heavy gauge polythene sheet to guard against moisture penetration, followed by a padded layer of felt paper, roofing felt, foam, cork-chipped sheet, building paper, or even carpet underlay.

The polythene is very important, even if the surface seems perfectly dry; solid strips in particular will warp at the slightest sign of dampness. The padded layer cushions the floor, takes up any slight unevenness, and protects the polythene from damage. Always follow the maker's recommendations on what material to use.

Suspended wooden floors don't need an underlay, but you should ensure the boarding is level and firmly fixed, and that all nails are punched down.

There is normally no need to line floorboards with hardboard. Double-check for evidence of structural dampness before laying over joists.

Where to start

Clear the room completely and decide where you are going to start. On a solid subfloor, boards are normally laid at right angles to the main window starting at the longest, straightest wall. On a suspended floor, lay them at right angles to the existing boards, or directly across the joists, starting from any convenient wall.

As with other floorcoverings, it's a good idea to lay out a row of strips across the room and check that you won't be left with a narrow gap on the far side. If necessary, trim the first row of strips lengthways to avoid this.

1 *Prise off skirtings with a bolster or crowbar, using a block of wood to protect the wall. Saw notches out of the door architraves to fit the strips.*

On a solid floor, overlap the sheets of polythene underlay by 100mm (4"). Carry them up the walls by the same amount and fasten temporarily with tape.

With the padded underlay in position, lay out the strips in a dry run across the room. If you're left with a narrow gap, trim down the first row.

PROBLEM SOLVER

Trimming woodstrip

Where you need to even up gaps, most types of woodstrip are easily cut along their length using a panel saw. For thicker solid strips, however, you'll find that a jigsaw and guide fence save a lot of effort.

Use a tenon saw to cut strips to fit around obstacles. The expansion gap around the edge of the floor gives you some manoeuvring room, but even so, it's safer to make a paper template of the area being filled than to rely on measuring.

Dealing with pipes

There are special techniques for cutting strips to fit around pipes and similar obstacles, depending on whether these fall at the end or side of a strip. In both cases, you'll need a flat bit which is fractionally larger than the pipes themselves.

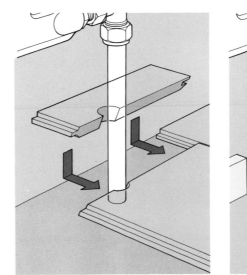
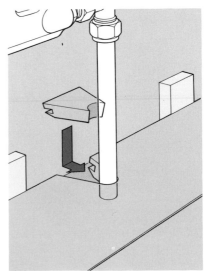

To fit around pipes begin by measuring and marking the exact position of the pipe on the panel or strip. Drill a hole at this point using a flat bit of slightly larger diameter.

Then, depending on whether the pipe is at the end (above) or side (above right), mark and saw out at notch as shown. Keep the offcut and glue in place after laying the whole strips.

LAMINATED PANELS: SOLID FLOOR

Laminated woodstrip panels are normally laid on solid floors using the 'floating floor' principle, in which only the joints are glued; the panels are not actually fixed to the floor at all. Use the same method for a hardboard or chipboard lined wooden floor, where nailing is difficult and unsatisfactory.

The secret of getting the panels to butt tightly together is to wedge them against the wall using offcuts of softwood the same thickness as the expansion gap. The wedges on one side of the room stay loose until you fit the last row of panels, at which point you can lever the panels together with a bolster or crowbar and fit more wedges to hold them tight. The wedges stay in place and are trimmed off later.

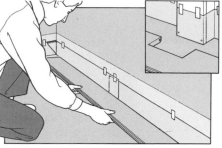

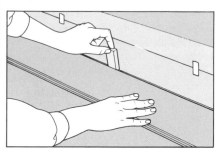

1 Position the first panel and check that the wall is relatively straight. If need be, scribe the panel to fit and plane along the marked line.

2 Position wedges along the wall then re-fit the panel against them leaving a 10mm (⅜") gap for expansion. Lay more panels in the same way.

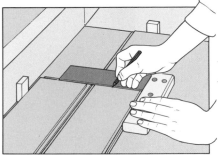

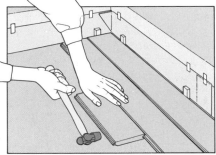

3 To trim the end panel, place it 'tongue to tongue' with the end butted to the wall as shown. Mark, then cut and fit. Glue the panel if recommended.

4 Use the offcut to start the next row, with the cut edge against the wall. Glue, then knock into place; use another offcut to protect the tongue.

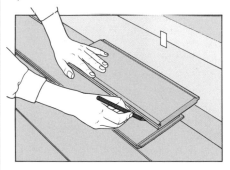

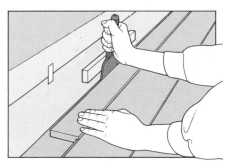

5 Continue laying panels in the same way. When you get to the last row, measure the remaining gap and then trim the panels 10mm (⅜") narrower.

6 Use a crowbar or bolster and a block of wood to lever the floor panels tightly together and drop in wooden wedges (two per panel) to lock them in place.

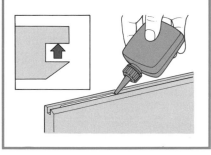
LAYING ON A SUSPENDED FLOOR

The technique for laying panels over boards or joists is the same as for a solid floor, except that you 'secret nail' through the tongues instead of gluing them. This gets round the need for wedges: each row is locked by the nails, so simply butt subsequent rows tightly.

Unless otherwise recommended, use oval wire nails twice the thickness of the flooring, Nail through the tongues at 300-500mm (12-20") intervals and punch the heads below the surface. On the last row, either glue the tongues or nail through the panels then punch and fill the holes.

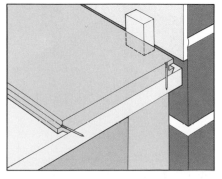

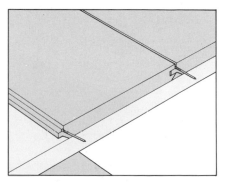

1 Fit the first row of panels with their grooved edge to the wall, using offcuts to create the expansion gap. Nail along the wall edge, then through the tongues.

2 Slot subsequent rows over the nailed tongues on the previous row, then nail their tongues. The last row can be glued, or nailed, and filled.

LAYING SOLID STRIPS WITH CLIPS

Again, the techniques for setting out, trimming and laying solid hardwood strips joined with a clip system are much the same as for laminated panels. The chief difference is the way the strips are fixed, which varies depending on the type of floor.

On a solid floor, wedge the strips together as previously described. Only the ends need gluing.

On a suspended floor – boards or joists – secret nail through the tongues in the normal way.

Solid strips look best if the joints are staggered, so set out each row in a dry run and cut strips short where necessary. There may also be some colour variation between strips, so make sure you lay them in a pleasingly random way.

Remember to insert the clips into the groove on the underside of the strips as you lay them, ready to receive the next row. Stagger the positions of the clips so that there's no danger of them fouling each other.

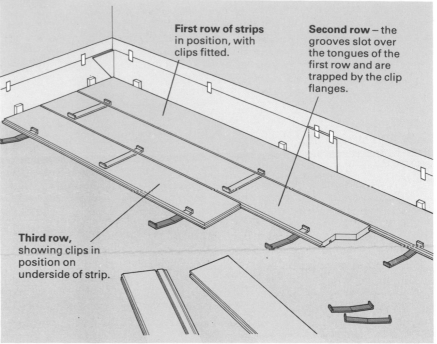

First row of strips in position, with clips fitted.

Second row – the grooves slot over the tongues of the first row and are trapped by the clip flanges.

Third row, showing clips in position on underside of strip.

Clip-together solid strips are designed to be locked together as they are laid. Fit the clips as you go, then slot in the next row of strips so that they are trapped by the flanges as shown.

FINISHING THE EDGES

With the floor in place, trim the wedges (where fitted) flush with the surface, then refit the skirtings, and make good. Where there are no skirtings, or you didn't remove them, pin quadrant or scotia moulding around the edges to hide the gaps. Punch down the nail heads and cover with wood filler.

There may also be doorways and steps to deal with. Most woodstrip ranges include special mouldings for dealing with such areas, though these may need cutting down or planing to fit the floorcoverings in other rooms.

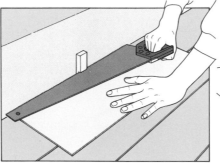

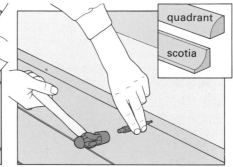

quadrant

scotia

Saw off any wedges flush with the surface of the floor using a panel saw. Place something underneath to prevent the woodstrip from being scratched.

If you cover the expansion gap with moulding, pin this to the wall or skirting (rather than the floor) to allow for movement. Punch the heads and cover with filler.

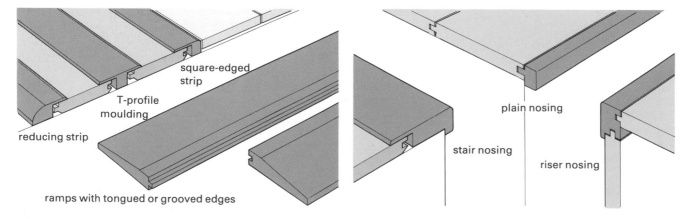

square-edged strip

T-profile moulding

reducing strip

ramps with tongued or grooved edges

plain nosing

stair nosing

riser nosing

Choose the appropriate threshold strip for the doorway, depending on the flooring in the next room and on the type of woodstrip laid. Some flooring systems include special threshold strips with tongued and grooved edges to match the strips.

Many ranges include mouldings for dealing with steps. Stop the flooring short of the step to allow for the width of the moulding and an expansion gap. For multiple steps, cover with woodstrip and pin moulding along the back. Paint the risers to match the wall.

LAYING SHEET VINYL FLOORING

Sheet vinyl flooring is ideal wherever you need a hardwearing, waterproof surface that's easy to keep clean and comfortable to walk on. This makes it a good choice not only for kitchens, bathrooms and halls, but for playrooms, dining areas and utility rooms as well.

There's a wide choice of patterns, ranging from plain geometric to simulated quarry tile and woodgrain. Most have some surface texture, and in the case of simulated types this is pronounced enough to give a realistic effect.

Sheet vinyl comes in widths of 2m (about 6'6"), 3m (9'9") and 4m (13'). This means that most rooms can be covered with one sheet – although sometimes it may be easier to join two narrower sheets.

Overleaf is a guide to estimating how much (and what width) to buy, depending on the shape of the room. But you may not find wider sheets in all patterns, so check availability before making a final choice.

There are two main types of vinyl, both of which come in a wide range of styles and patterns:
Unbacked vinyl consists of a single layer of solid vinyl; only the thicker types are textured. Most unbacked vinyls won't lay flat naturally and must be glued to the floor.
Cushioned vinyl consists of multiple layers, the most important of which is a foam backing that makes it softer and warmer to walk on in bare feet. The surface is usually textured.

Some cushioned vinyl is designed to lay flat naturally and doesn't need gluing. (One exception is under a heavy kitchen appliance, such as a cooker, where gluing stops the vinyl dragging if the appliance has to be moved.) Non-'lay flat' types only need to be glued near the edges and along any joins.
Other materials: If the vinyl needs sticking down, check the maker's instructions for details of suitable adhesives. Most types come with a spreader.

Seam adhesive gives a professional finish to joins between sheets (see page 72).

Adhesive tape is essential for several stages, and you may need metal cover strips for doorways. Use brown wrapping paper or heavy lining paper to make templates (see page 71).
Tools checklist: Trimming knife, soft broom, metal rule or straight edge, blocks of wood. (Extra tools are needed if the floor has to be prepared first – see overleaf.)

Cross-sections of unbacked vinyl and a typical cushioned vinyl.

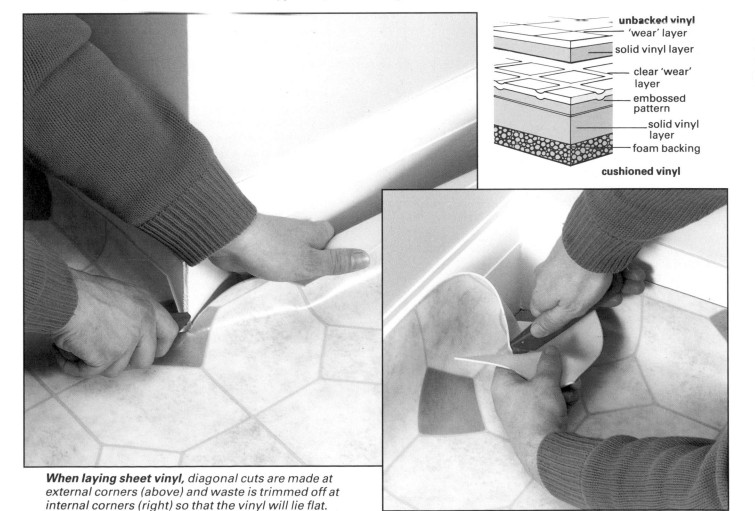

When laying sheet vinyl, diagonal cuts are made at external corners (above) and waste is trimmed off at internal corners (right) so that the vinyl will lie flat.

unbacked vinyl
'wear' layer
solid vinyl layer
clear 'wear' layer
embossed pattern
solid vinyl layer
foam backing

cushioned vinyl

PREPARATION AND PLANNING

The plans given here show what's involved in laying sheet vinyl in three different situations. Start by seeing what needs to be done to the existing floor surface, then work out the best way to lay the sheet.

Preparing the floor

Vinyl must only be laid on a surface which is even, clean and dry. Any bumps or hollows will eventually show through, and damp can damage a cushioned backing as well as being a problem in its own right.

Floorboards Level old pine boarded floors with sheets of hardboard. With new boards or chipboard, ensure all nail heads are punched below the surface, fill any gaps with general purpose filler, and vacuum.

Concrete Make sure the floor is not damp. If the surface is smooth but dusty, vacuum and apply a coat of concrete sealer; if it is uneven, level with self-smoothing compound.

Quarry/ceramic tiles Check that the tiles are securely fixed and level the joints with filler.

Old glued floor coverings Lift old lino or felt backed vinyl; to remove any remaining backing felt, soak with one part household ammonia to three of water and scrape off.

Old vinyl tiles can stay if firmly fixed; otherwise warm with a hot air stripper to soften the adhesive and lift, scraping off all traces of old adhesive. Old thermoplastic tiles discolour vinyl sheet, so either lift them or screed over the top with latex-based self-smoothing compound.

In all cases it's a good idea to remove inward opening doors and trim the undersides.

Planning how much to buy

Measure the maximum width and length of the room – going right into any recesses or door openings – then draw a sketch plan and put in the dimensions. Take the longest and widest measurements and add 200mm (8″) for a trimming allowance on each side. This represents the minimum sheet size needed to fill the room.

Aim to choose a width that allows you to cover the whole area with a single piece. (If the room is seriously out of square, allow extra for trimming or you may get caught out.) Most stockists sell in lengths to the nearest metre or half metre so you may end up with a bit extra.

Where the size or shape of the room makes it impossible to use a single piece, use your plan to work out the best way of fitting in two or more pieces bearing in mind the following points:

■ Joins between sheets tend to lift and curl in time, so place them where they won't receive heavy wear.

■ A join which runs at right angles to the main light source is less noticeable than one running parallel.

■ It's not normally a good idea to use sheets of different widths on the same floor – they will have been made on a different run and are seldom an exact colour match. However, you can save a lot of wastage this way, especially if the second piece is small and not in a prominent place.

■ Allow extra overlap between pieces for matching the pattern. Makers normally specify the size of the pattern repeat.

EXAMPLE 1: A REGULARLY SHAPED ROOM

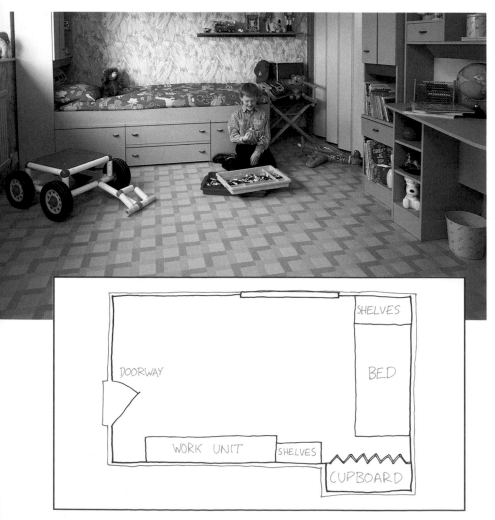

Most rooms are fairly regular in shape with no awkward areas, except perhaps a chimney breast. Providing the maximum width is less than 4m (13′) you should be able to use a single piece.

If you choose a vinyl with an irregular pattern, it won't matter if the walls are slightly out of true. Otherwise, take into account that the pattern must line up with the longest wall or dominant feature (eg a run of kitchen units), or the floor won't look 'right'.

And if the vinyl has a large pattern, like tile squares, it's a good idea to allow extra for trimming so that you can balance the breaks in the pattern between all sides of the room – small slivers of pattern always look like patched mistakes.

A rectangular room with few obstructions (above) can usually be covered in one piece. Check this by drawing a sketch plan (left), not forgetting to allow extra where the sheet has to fit into alcoves and doorways. Lay the vinyl by unrolling it in the room and trimming the sides to fit each wall in turn.

EXAMPLE 2: A THROUGH ROOM

If you want to lay vinyl in two connected areas, such as a kitchen and breakfast room, you have two choices:

■ Lay a single piece trimmed to fit both rooms and the partition between them. This can be tricky – especially if there is a narrow opening or a thick partition – and is only feasible if the maximum width of the area (plus trimming allowance) is less than 4m (13′).

■ Lay two pieces with a join between the rooms or in a convenient area of one of them. This is less neat, and it can be hard to match the pattern, but it's much easier to do.

In an L-shaped through room, like the one shown, it's tempting to place the join across the partition. But a better solution in this case is to lay a single piece over the part receiving the heaviest wear – usually the area between two doorways – then fit a second piece in the corner which gets used the least. A sensible furniture arrangement may help here.

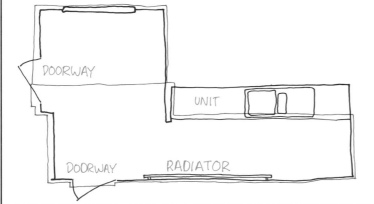

An L-shaped through room (above) poses the problem of what width to buy and where to place the joins. Try out different layouts on a sketch plan (left).

Here, the most economical way is to cover the area between the doorways with one piece, then fit a second in the relatively unused area by the dining table. If the kitchen were wider, it might be possible to cover both rooms with a single piece.

EXAMPLE 3: AN OBSTACLE-FILLED ROOM

Some rooms are an awkward shape or full of obstacles, such as a small bathroom with a toilet, pedestal basin and towel rail. In these situations, it's very difficult to lay vinyl directly and cut round the various shapes.

A better method is to make a paper template of the whole area, showing the obstacles, and use this as a pattern to cut the sheet before you fit it (see page 71). However, don't use this method for a room larger than a couple of metres square, as the template is unlikely to be accurate enough. Instead, unfurl the vinyl in the room as best you can, then make separate templates of the obstacles.

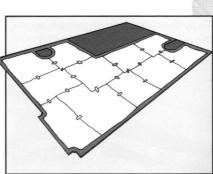

In small rooms full of obstacles, it's easier to cut the vinyl following a paper pattern. Cut on the generous side, then do a final trim with the sheet in position.

JOINS, EDGES AND FINISHING

Where you need to join sheets, start by scribing and direct-timming the first sheet to fit. Leave plenty of overlap along the joining edge so that you can match the pattern.

After matching and trimming the join with the second sheet as shown, stick down the edges with a 150mm (6") band of adhesive (see below) before you trim the rest of the second sheet to fit. This stops it slipping out of position.

At doorways, take care to cut the overlap to the full width of the doorway – not just the width of the door stop in the middle. Finish the join between the two coverings with an aluminium cover strip.

Gluing and finishing

Unbacked vinyl must be glued all over. Spread the adhesive over half the floor following the maker's instructions, lay the trimmed sheet lightly in position, then smooth out towards the edges with a soft broom to remove air bubbles. Repeat for the other part of the floor.

Cushioned vinyl normally only needs sticking down with a 150mm (6") band of adhesive at joins, but glue it all over where it is laid under heavy appliances. Both jobs can be done with the sheet in position.

Afterwards, smooth down the glued areas with a piece of wood wrapped in a soft cloth.

At doorways, fit a metal cover strip with a ramp to match the thickness of the floorcovering in the adjoining room. Nail or screw the strip in place over the vinyl.

1 *To join two pieces,* fit the first sheet and lay the second on top. Align their patterns, leaving at least 100mm (4") overlap on the opposite wall.

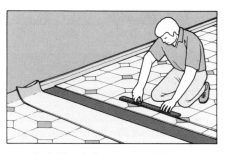

2 Fold back the second sheet and choose where to make the join (a 'line' in the pattern is ideal). Mark this line and cut along it against a straight edge.

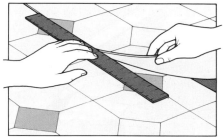

3 Tuck the second sheet under the first sheet. Butt a straight edge against the trimmed edge, fold back this edge, then cut the second sheet.

■ PROBLEM SOLVER ■

Tight fits

Trimmed edges sometimes become a tight fit along walls as the sheet begins to settle and flatten. If this happens, mark where the sheet fits perfectly on either side of the problem area, then fold back the sheet and join the marks with a straight line. Re-trim along this line using a straightedge.

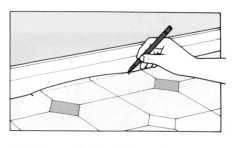

Marking a tightly fitting edge.

Accidental cuts

If the knife slips or you cut in the wrong place, repair the cut with non-stain double sided tape and seaming adhesive – both available from vinyl suppliers.

Cut a length of tape and run the sticky side down the cut on the underside of the sheet. Remove the backing from the tape and press down the sheet.

Now run a thin bead of seaming adhesive along the full length of the cut so that it just fills it. The adhesive will bond the edges together so that they are barely noticeable.

Patch cuts with double sided tape and seaming adhesive.

Sheet overtrimmed

When you've fitted the first edge and come to trim the second, you still have room for manoeuvre if you trim too much: slide the sheet along a bit, scribe the first edge again, then re-trim.

If the problem occurs after you have fitted two or more edges and you're left with an unsightly gap, one answer is to pin softwood quadrant moulding around the skirting or wall to disguise it (see below).

Alternatively, patch in a strip using tape and seaming adhesive. Disguise the join in the patch by running it along a line in the pattern.

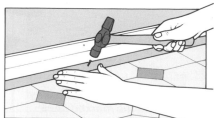

Hide gaps with quadrant moulding.

BOARDING A LOFT

One of the most important steps towards making more use of the space in a loft or attic is to lay a firm floor. Depending on the situation, this may be straightforward, or it could involve a fair amount of structural work. So the first thing to do is ask yourself what you hope to gain:

Extra storage only? If you don't intend turning the loft into a 'habitable' space – ie a bedroom or living room – you won't be bound by Building Regulations or Planning Acts. In most cases a loft used for storage or as a playroom will carry only light loads; it is unlikely to need structural modification and can simply be covered with suitable boarding. However, if you are putting anything heavy on the floor, you may need to reinforce the structure (see below).

Extra living space? Loft conversions intended to create habitable rooms need Building Regulations approval, and may require Planning Permission. Because of the extra loads imposed by new rooms, it's essential that the new floor is strong enough to take the weight before boarding.

Surveying the loft

With the above in mind, inspect the structural woodwork in the roof space. At the same time, check whether there is any insulation, pipework or wiring which could interfere with your plans.

How you proceed depends on the size of the joists. Normally, these are only intended to support the ceiling below, plus the odd fitting such as a cold storage tank. Even so, some ceiling joists – particularly in older houses – are substantial enough to take the load of a new room as well (see overleaf).

Where the original joists aren't strong enough, you have to reinforce them in some way prior to boarding (leaving the original ceiling unaffected). This involves much more complication and expense, and should only be considered as part of a complete loft conversion. It is essential to employ a professional to carry out the design and specification of the structural alterations, but you can save money by doing the woodwork yourself.

A loft floor can be made from a variety of materials. One of the simplest methods is to use purpose-made panels of flooring grade chipboard, specially designed to make the job cheap, quick and simple.

....Shopping List....

Flooring boards can be made from flooring grade chipboard or softwood (see overleaf for details of these options). As your choice of material affects how you lay it and therefore the amount of wastage, it may be worth drawing a sketch plan of the area you want to board to help work out exactly how much to buy.

Nails For chipboard, use *annular ring shank* nails about 2½ times the board's thickness – eg 50mm (2″) nails for 19mm (¾″) flooring. You need about 7 nails per metre length of each joist you nail to, plus plenty of extras for odd corners and added supports. For floorboards, use *cut*

floorboard or *oval wire* nails – about 12 per metre length of joist.

Screws Use 38mm (1½″) No.8 countersunk woodscrews to fix panels over pipes and wires which you may need to reach for maintenance.

Extra supports Lengths of 100×50mm (4×2″), 75×50mm (3×2″), 50×50mm (2×2″) and 50×25mm (2×1″) sawn timber battens will come in useful for supporting cut ends and access panels. Lay on a supply of 75mm (3″) oval nails for fixing them.

Tools checklist: Saw, hammer, screwdriver, chisel, straightedge, plane, tape measure, pencil.

CHECKING THE JOISTS

Inspect the timbers all round the roof space to ensure that they are sound and not suffering from rot or woodworm. Then measure them.

The size of joist needed to support a normally loaded floor depends on how much space there is between the joists and how far they have to span between supports. The calculations are complicated, so if there is any doubt about this side of the job, consult a professional.

As a rough guide, the following table shows the maximum allowable span for joists spaced at the usual 400mm (16″) between centres, and at a spacing of 600mm (24″):

Joist size	Max span at 400mm (16″)	Max span at 600mm (24″)
125×38mm (5×1½″)	2.2m (7′2″)	–
150×38mm (6×1½″)	2.8m (9′2″)	2.2m (7′2″)
175×38mm (7×1½″)	3.2m (10′6″)	2.6m (8′6″)
200×38mm (8×1½″)	3.6m (11′9″)	3.0m (9′10″)
125×44mm (5×1¾″)	2.4m (7′10″)	–
150×44mm (6×1¾″)	3.0m (9′10″)	2.4m (7′10″)
175×44mm (7×1¾″)	3.4m (11′2″)	2.8m (9′2″)
200×44mm (8×1¾″)	4.0m (13′2″)	3.2m (10′6″)
100×50mm (4×2″)	2.0m (6′7″)	–
125×50mm (5×2″)	2.6m (8′6″)	2.0m (6′7″)
150×50mm (6×2″)	3.2m (10′6″)	2.6m (8′6″)
175×50mm (7×2″)	3.6m (11′9″)	3.0m (9′10″)
200×50mm (8×2″)	4.0m (13′2″)	3.4m (11′2″)

Where the joists are too small, there are three ways to provide extra support as shown below:
■ Strengthen the existing joists by bolting on new or top members.
■ Add new, larger joists between the old ones. These can rest on the same loadbearing walls, or (if only part of the loft is to be floored) on new beams carried by the walls.
■ Support the joists with beams fitted below the ceiling. This is usually a last resort where the loft floor cannot be raised as in the other two methods.

In each case, seek professional advice on the size of joists and method of support. Structural alterations to the roof require approval from the local authority Building Control Office.

PARTIAL NEW JOISTS

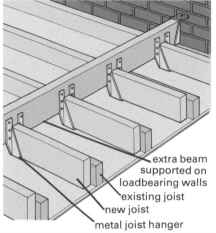

extra beam supported on loadbearing walls
existing joist
new joist
metal joist hanger

FULL-LENGTH NEW JOISTS

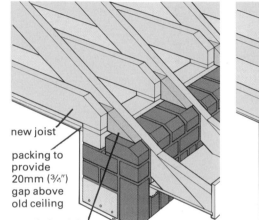

new joist
packing to provide 20mm (¾″) gap above old ceiling
existing joist

SUPPORTING BEAMS

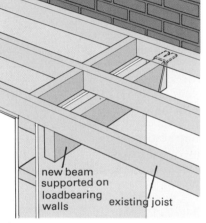

new beam supported on loadbearing walls
existing joist

PREPARATION

The following measures should ensure that the job goes smoothly:
■ Lay on extra lighting by running an extension lead from a downstairs socket to power inspection lamps. A spotlight with a clip to fit the rafters is useful for working under the eaves.
■ Provide good access. If you are planning to fit a loft ladder, do this first. Otherwise, use a sturdy ladder tied off to the hatch so that you can manhandle the boards without risk of slipping off.
■ Arrange a platform to work from until the boards are in place – it's all too easy to put a foot wrong and step between the joists, damaging the ceiling (and possibly yourself). If you are laying floorboards, use a piece of chipboard or plywood.
■ Clear junk from around the joists, then vacuum up any dust and debris. If you need to handle insulation materials, wear a dust mask, goggles and gloves.

Where there are things that can't be moved temporarily, stack them to one side, well away from where you intend to start working.

Before laying the boards, clear the loft and arrange easy access. You also need to deal with any services (pipes or cables) and insulation material which is in the way of the new floor.

Run an extension lead from below to provide extra light, hooking up the flex so it doesn't trail across the working area.

Fit a loft ladder or tie off a conventional ladder to the hatch to provide a safe means of access.

FLOORING OPTIONS

Flooring grade chipboard (often marked *Type II* or *BS 5669)* is the cheapest option, being much stronger than ordinary chipboard. For a joist spacing of under 450mm (18"), use the widely available 19mm (¾") thickness; for wider spacings use 22mm (⅞") board.

Standard sheets of chipboard measuring 2440×1220mm (8×4') are too large to pass through a loft hatch and need cutting down. Narrower panels are made specially for boarding a loft; these are either 400mm (16") or 610mm (2') wide and 1220mm (4') or 2440mm (8') long. Most panels have tongued and grooved (T&G) edges. Square edged boards need extra support between joists.

Softwood floorboards are more expensive and take longer to lay than chipboard, but they are better looking and can be easier to handle. Normal sizes are 100 or 150mm (4 or 6") wide in various stock lengths – commonly 3.0m (10'). Thickness varies from 19mm (¾") to 25mm (1"); use the latter where the joist spacing is 450mm (18") or more.

Floorboards may be square edged or tongued and grooved (T&G). T&G is slightly more expensive but makes a sturdier floor.

Square-edged flooring grade chipboard comes in large sheets which need cutting down.

Tongued and grooved flooring grade chipboard comes in easily manageable panels.

Floorboards come with either square or T&G edges. Though easy to handle, they are more costly.

Notch the joists to set pipes or cables below the level of the new floor. Metal plates reinforce the joists and protect against accidental puncturing.

Old insulation only needs removing if you are making a habitable space, or where it interferes with laying the boards.

Dealing with obstacles

Old insulation is messy to remove, and unless you are converting the loft into habitable space there is little harm in boarding over the top; the only effect will be to reduce the amount of heat rising from below. Where the insulation is deeper than the joists, soft fibre material should simply compress down – although it's as well to check first; polystyrene sheet, mineral wool and loose fill must be trimmed level with the joists.

If you intend to heat the loft it must be insulated at rafter level instead (see Problem Solver). Take up the old insulation and pack it in polythene bags for disposal – or re-use if it is worth salvaging.

Pipes and cables running over joists must be notched into them instead. This weakens the timber somewhat, so take care not to cut any deeper than necessary.

There is also a risk of nailing through notched pipes and cables when laying the boards. Guard against this – and reinforce the joists – by screwing metal plates over the notches.

LAYING CHIPBOARD

Because of their size, chipboard sheets and panels are quick to lay, but you need plenty of clear space to work in. And because all square-cut edges must be supported by the joists or by extra *noggins*, it's worth drawing a plan showing where the boards are to fit (this also helps you gauge how much to buy).

■ The laying pattern depends on whether you are using T&G or square-edged boards. In both cases, you must lay the boards in an overlapping pattern (like bricks) so that the end joints do not line up. The diagrams on the right show how to arrange each type.

■ Both types of board will need some cutting to suit the layout. Chipboard can be cut with any sort of hand or power saw, but will quickly blunt the blade unless you use one with hardened teeth.

Plan the job to avoid unnecessary cutting. In the case of joists spaced at 400mm (16″) centres, you can get by with very little – the standard lengths of boards can be arranged to fall conveniently on top of the joist positions.

At the same time, work out the positions of panels that need to be removable for access to services. These may require extra noggins to fit them comfortably into the plan.

Preparing the chipboard

When you buy the boards, stack them flat in a pile indoors until you are ready to use them – don't lean them against a wall or keep them outdoors as they may warp. The boards should be 'conditioned' by laying them out loosely in the loft for a day or two before fitting. This will allow them to adjust to the temperature and moisture in the air, helping to minimize warping or shrinkage later.

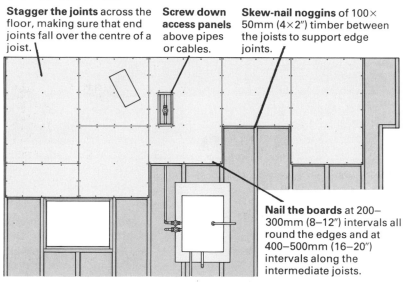

Stagger the joints across the floor, making sure that end joints fall over the centre of a joist.

Nail the boards along the centre line of each joist. Put one nail near each side of the sheet and two equally spaced in the middle.

Where you need access to pipes or cables, fit noggins to support an access panel on all four sides. Remove the tongues from the panel and screw in place.

T&G floor panels are laid across the joists so that their ends meet over a joist. The long edges do not require extra support, but gluing the tongues and grooves with PVA adhesive helps to lock them together and stiffen up the floor as a whole.

Stagger the joints across the floor, making sure that end joints fall over the centre of a joist.

Screw down access panels above pipes or cables.

Skew-nail noggins of 100× 50mm (4×2″) timber between the joists to support edge joints.

Nail the boards at 200–300mm (8–12″) intervals all round the edges and at 400–500mm (16–20″) intervals along the intermediate joists.

Square-edged boards cut down from a sheet are laid parallel to the joists so that their long edges meet over a joist. Noggins must be fitted between the joists so that the ends of both boards are supported wherever there is a joint.

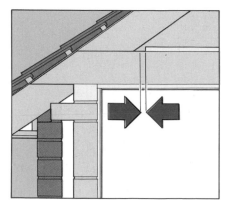

If you are boarding the whole loft, start in one corner (for T&G boards, place the tongued sides against the wall). Leave a gap of about 10mm (½″) along the eaves.

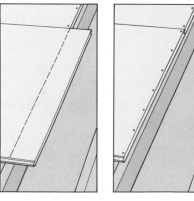

Where the edge of a board overlaps a joist, rule a line along it coinciding with the centre of the joist. Saw along this line and nail to the joist.

Square-cut edges which don't fall over joists must be supported by noggins. Cut the noggins slightly oversize, knock into place and skew-nail to the joists.

LAYING FLOORBOARDS

Floorboards are laid across the joists in more or less continuous strips, so unlike chipboard sheets or panels, there is no need to plan where each board is to go. The only point to watch is that all end-to-end joints fall over a joist so that both ends are supported.

To work out how many boards you need, measure the width of the floor in line with the joists and divide this by the width of a board; if you are using T&G floorboards, remember to deduct the width of

the tongue – about 10mm (³⁄₈″).

Multiply the result by the dimensions of the floor across the joists to get total length of boarding needed. Then add on extra to allow for having to cut standard lengths to fit – the actual amount depends on how much cutting you anticipate having to do.

Spread the boards out loosely in the loft to condition for at least a week before laying. If you have to saw boards shorter to get them through the loft hatch, cut them to

the longest possible length that will fit the loft space conveniently and span a whole number of joists.

The fact that the boards are narrow means that you can lift them individually for access to services. However, if you are using T&G it is quite tricky to separate the tongued and grooved edges, so where there are services which you might need to reach frequently it's worth fitting a removable panel instead. This can be the width of a single board, or it can span a number of them.

1 Lay the first board in place, leaving a 10mm (½″) gap along the eaves (with T&G, put the tongued side to the wall). Mark across the board in line with the centre of the last joist it crosses. Saw across the board at this point.

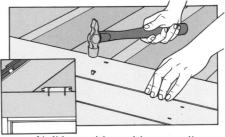

2 Nail in position with two nails into each alternate joist. Put the nails about 25mm (1″) from the edges of the board and near the centre line of the joist.

3 Use a bolster to lever subsequent boards tightly against their neighbours. If you have a lot of boards to lay, you can hire a special flooring cramp.

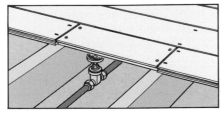

The simplest way to make an access panel the width of one board is to saw the board across the centres of two joists and screw down both ends.

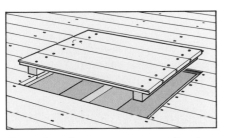

To make a larger access panel, cut a number of short lengths to span from joist to joist. Join the boards together with battens screwed to the underside.

With T&G boards, you can arrange for an access panel to be lifted easily by removing the lower side of the grooved edge. Do this with a chisel or plane, as shown. Afterwards, fix the panel to the joists using countersunk screws.

Insulating the roof

If you want the loft space to be warmed by heat rising from the rooms below – or the loft itself is to be heated – it must be insulated at rafter level rather than between the joists. Where the loft space is to form a habitable room, minimum standards of insulation are laid down by the Building Regulations.

Normally, the simplest option is to fit 100mm (4″) of insulation between the rafters as shown, leaving an air gap of around 50mm (2″) between this and the roof covering. Provide a similar sized air gap along the eaves – for example, by fitting plastic eaves vents.

Glass fibre or mineral wool matting are both suitable, but expanded polystyrene sheets or mineral wool batts are easier to handle. You also need a vapour barrier to protect the rafters from condensation: use polythene sheet if you plan to line the roof, otherwise a thick grade of building paper looks better and is more robust.

Use the vapour barrier to trap the insulation in place. Cut the sheet into convenient widths. Then, starting from the bottom, staple or tack it to the rafters and slip in the insulation as you go.

Insulate at roof level to keep the loft space warm. You can use any rigid or semi-rigid type of loft insulation materials.

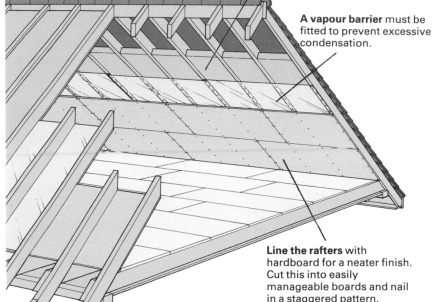

Insulation can be fitted between the rafters. Make sure there is a 50mm (2″) air gap under the roof covering and provide ventilation along the eaves.

A vapour barrier must be fitted to prevent excessive condensation.

Line the rafters with hardboard for a neater finish. Cut this into easily manageable boards and nail in a staggered pattern.

Lining the roof

In a full loft conversion, the rafters would be lined with plasterboard or wood cladding – possibly with a false ceiling and walls to avoid awkward corners around the eaves and ridge. But for storage purposes, you can fit a lightweight lining of hardboard instead.

Cut full-size sheets into manageable lengths which fit exactly between rafter centres. Fit them in a staggered pattern, like floor panels, nailing at 150mm (6″) intervals.

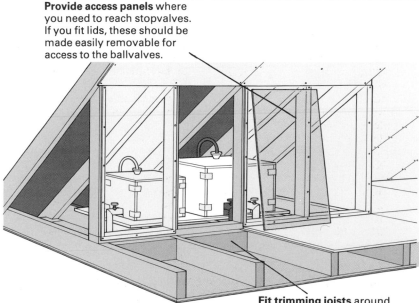

Provide access panels where you need to reach stopvalves. If you fit lids, these should be made easily removable for access to the ballvalves.

Fit trimming joists around tanks to support the new floor. Cut the boards so that they stop just short of the tanks, then nail them to the trimmers.

Don't board under a tank. If it is obtrusive or vulnerable, box it in with chipboard panels – but make sure it remains easily accessible for maintenance.

Dealing with water tanks

In many lofts a considerable amount of space is devoted to the cold water storage tank – and possibly a central heating expansion tank as well. A full loft conversion is quite likely to involve moving the tanks, but for simple storage purposes the amount of work involved is normally unjustified – it's better simply to disguise and protect them.

Whatever you do, it's important not to block off the area below the tanks since heat rising helps to prevent them from freezing in cold weather. You also need free access to the stopvalves fitted in this area.

Often the neatest way to disguise a tank is to box it in with chipboard panels and insulate behind. Make the top removable, and create separate access panels for the valves.

INDEX

ACKNOWLEDGEMENTS

Photographers

Aaronson 73; Amtico 45(t), 45(c), 48; Cristal Tiles 10-11, 14;
Decorwool Carpets front cover(tl); Dunlop 39; Eaglemoss (Jon
Bouchier) 7, 9, 12-13, 14(inset), 15-17, 19-22, (Derek St Romaine)
25, 54, (Steve Tanner) 23(b), 27(r), 29-30, 35, 37(t), 40, 47, 57(b),
60-62, 67, 75, 77; Fired Earth front cover(br), 1(tl); Forbo Nairn
68-69; Gripperods 51-52; H & R Johnstone 32(l); Halsteads 42-43;
Robert Harding Picture Library 1(br), 2; Huega 41, 43; Ideal
Standard 6; I.W.S 49; Langley 27(l); Pilkingtons 23(t); SIC/Marie
Claire 46; Syndication International 45(b); Tarkett 63; Texas 59(l);
Tile Lines front cover(bl); Elizabeth Whiting Associates 4, 31(r),
32(r), 33, 57(t); Wickes 31(l), 37(b), 59(r).

Illustrators

Kuo Kang Chen 49-52, 67-72; Paul Emra 9-14, 15-18, 19-22;
Jeremy Gower 7-8; Andrew Green 37-40, 53-56, 59-62, 64-66, 74-
78; Alex Jessel 19-22; Maltings Partnership front cover(tr), 41-44;
Fraser Newman 9-14; Stan North 23-26, 28-30, 31-36, 45-48;
David Weeks 7-8; Paul Williams 58.